NEW MEXICO

TRAVEL GUIDE

2023

"Encounter the Spirit of New Mexico: Festivals, Art, Culinary Delights, Top Attractions, History, and Culture" as well as "Enjoying Your Stay Like a Pro"

By

ROY ORTIZ

TABLE OF CONTENT

Chapter 12: Practical Information for new Mexico visitors

A. Currency and exchange rates

B. Health and safety tips

C. Communication and internet access

D. Useful phrases in Spanish

E. Recap of why New Mexico is a great travel destination

F. Useful apps and websites to enhance your New Mexico travel experience

Introduction

I knew my New Mexico vacation would be unforgettable as soon as I stepped off the plane and felt the warm desert breeze. The vivid colors of the landscape and the state's rich cultural heritage immediately captivated my senses.

My journey began in Albuquerque, where I immersed myself in the vibrant atmosphere of the city. I strolled through the cobblestone streets of Old Town, admiring the adobe architecture. As I ate delicious New Mexican cuisine at local restaurants, the scent of green chile lingered in the air.

I got up early one morning to see the spectacular Albuquerque International Balloon Fiesta. The sky was filled with colorful hot air balloons floating gracefully over the Sandia Mountains. It was a breathtaking sight, and I couldn't resist taking a hot air balloon ride myself. Soaring above the Rio

Grande Valley, I marveled at the panoramic views of the sprawling city and the picturesque landscape below.

I left Albuquerque and headed to Santa Fe, New Mexico's enchanting capital. The city's art scene was a visual feast, with numerous galleries displaying traditional and contemporary works. I spent hours exploring the Georgia O'Keeffe Museum, immersing myself in the vibrant colors and captivating landscapes of her paintings.

One evening, I went to the Santa Fe Plaza, the cultural hub of the city. While I browsed the stalls of local artisans selling handmade jewelry, pottery, and textiles, street performers entertained the crowds. I couldn't help but buy a beautiful piece of turquoise jewelry as a souvenir of my trip.

The next day, I set out on a scenic drive along the Turquoise Trail, which winds through majestic mountains and quaint mining towns. The rugged landscapes and deep blue skies awed me at every turn. I stopped in Madrid, where I explored the eclectic art galleries and ate a delicious meal at a charming café.

Continuing on my journey, I arrived in Taos, a town known for its artistic community and Native American heritage. I went to Taos Pueblo, a UNESCO World Heritage Site, and marveled at the ancient adobe buildings while learning about the Native American community's rich history. The powwow, with its vibrant dances and mesmerizing drumming, was a highlight of my visit.

No trip to New Mexico would be complete without exploring its natural wonders. I hiked through the rugged canyons of Bandelier National Monument, following in the footsteps of ancient civilizations and exploring the cliff dwellings carved into the rock formations.

As my New Mexico vacation came to an end, I reflected on the incredible experiences and memories I had made. The state's diverse landscapes, rich culture, and warm hospitality left an indelible imprint on my heart. New Mexico truly lived up to its reputation as the Land of Enchantment, and I knew I would treasure these memories for the rest of my life.

New Mexico is a state in the southwestern United States with a rich cultural past, spectacular natural landscapes, and a diverse population. Because of its mesmerizing beauty, strong customs, and historical significance, it is known as the Land of Enchantment. Let's start with an overview of New Mexico, looking at its geography, history, culture, and prominent attractions.

New Mexico shares geographical borders with Arizona, Colorado, Oklahoma, Texas, and Utah, as well as Mexico to the south. The state's topography is diverse, ranging from scorching deserts and mesas to snow-capped mountains and deep canyons. The Rio Grande, one of North America's longest rivers, flows through the state's center, altering the terrain and providing water for cultivation.

New Mexico has an interesting history that predates European settlement. Native American groups such as the Navajo, Apache, Pueblo, and others have lived in the area for thousands of years. In the 16th century, Spanish explorers arrived and established Santa Fe as the capital of the province of Santa Fe de Nuevo México. Over time, New Mexico became a cultural crossroads, with influences from Native American, Spanish, Mexican, and Anglo-American traditions.

New Mexico's lively arts, food, and festivals have been shaped by its diverse cultural mix. The state is well-known for its art culture, particularly in Santa Fe, which is home to a plethora of galleries, museums, and art festivals. The cuisine of New Mexico is a delectable combination of flavors that draws inspiration from Native American, Mexican, and Spanish culinary traditions. Green and red chile sauces, enchiladas, tamales, and sopapillas are all iconic foods.

The amazing natural beauty of New Mexico is one of its most noteworthy features. Several national parks, monuments, and wilderness areas can be found in the state. The huge stretches of sparkling white gypsum dunes at White Sands National Park create a bizarre and magnificent landscape. Carlsbad Caverns National Park is known for its extensive underground cave system, which is ornamented with stalagmites and stalactites. The Bisti/De-Na-Zin Wilderness, Bandelier National Monument, and the gorgeous Sangre de Cristo Range are among the other natural treasures.

New Mexico is also well-known for its diverse cultural heritage and historical landmarks. Taos Pueblo, a UNESCO World Heritage Site, is one of the United States' oldest continuously inhabited towns, with adobe structures dating back over 1,000 years. Albuquerque holds the annual International Balloon Fiesta, where hundreds of colorful hot air balloons fill the sky in a spectacular spectacle.

In addition to its cultural and environmental attractions, New Mexico is home to notable scientific and research institutes such as Los Alamos National Laboratory and the Very Large Array of the National Radio Astronomy Observatory. These organizations have made significant contributions to the advancement of scientific knowledge and exploration.

Whether you're looking for outdoor adventures, ancient cultures, delectable cuisine, or to immerse yourself in art and history, New Mexico has something for everyone. Its stunning vistas, kind friendliness, and cultural wealth make it an intriguing location worth visiting.

A. Geography and Climate

The topography and climate of New Mexico contribute to its distinct and diversified scenery.

Geographically, New Mexico is a land of opposites. The state is the fifth largest in the United States, with an area of approximately 121,590 square miles (314,917 square kilometers). Its topography ranges from deserts and craggy mountains to wide plateaus and deep valleys.

The Colorado Plateau, to the west, is distinguished by mesas, canyons, and sandstone formations. The southern Rocky Mountains, notably the Sangre de Cristo Range, dominate the state's central and northern regions. This rugged region is home to numerous peaks above 13,000 feet (3,962 meters), including Wheeler Peak, New Mexico's highest point at 13,167 feet (4,013 meters).

The southern section of the state is predominantly desert topography, with huge areas of parched plains, sand dunes, and desert basins. The world's largest gypsum sand dune field can be found in White Sands National Park, which is located in this region.

Because of its unique landscape and elevation fluctuations, the climate of New Mexico differs greatly across the state. In general, the state has a high desert environment with little humidity, plentiful sunshine, and huge temperature changes.

Summers in the southern and central deserts are hot and dry, with temperatures frequently topping 100°F (38°C). Winters are moderate during the day but can be cool at night, with snowfall in some locations. Northern mountainous regions have a cooler and more alpine climate, with milder summers and colder winters. Higher elevations in the mountains receive more precipitation, including snowfall during the winter months.

The existence of the Rio Grande, which runs through the state's central region, mitigates the state's arid climate and limited rainfall. The river and its tributaries offer water for agriculture, irrigation, and recreation, while also supporting lush valleys and verdant vistas along their journey.

The unique topography and climate of New Mexico provide a wide choice of outdoor activities, from hiking and skiing in the mountains to exploring desert vistas and enjoying water sports along the Rio Grande. The state's natural splendor and diverse ecosystems make it an enticing destination for nature lovers and outdoor explorers.

B. History and Culture

New Mexico has a rich history and lively culture that have been influenced by a kaleidoscope of Native American, Spanish, Mexican, and Anglo-American influences.

For thousands of years, Native American tribes have lived in what is now New Mexico. The Pueblo people, which include the Hopi, Zuni, Acoma, and Taos tribes, have significant ancestral ties to the area. Their exquisite adobe houses, cliff homes, and ceremonial sites remain evidence of their past civilizations. Taos Pueblo, a UNESCO World Heritage Site, is one of the United States' oldest continuously inhabited towns, with multi-story adobe buildings dating back over 1,000 years.

Spanish adventurers led by Francisco Vázquez de Coronado visited the region in the 16th century in pursuit of legendary gold cities. Santa Fe, the state capital, was founded by the Spanish in 1610, making it the oldest capital city in the United States. Over the decades that followed, Spanish influence impacted the region's culture, architecture, and traditions, with adobe-style houses and Catholic missions becoming iconic emblems of the region.

Mexico declared independence from Spain in 1821, and New Mexico became a Mexican territory. However, as part of the Treaty of Guadalupe Hidalgo, the United States gained possession of New Mexico during the Mexican-American War of 1846–1848. During this time, the region saw an influx of Anglo-American settlers.

The blending of Native American, Spanish, Mexican, and Anglo-American cultures in New Mexico has resulted in a unique cultural synthesis. Through different festivals, art forms, and culinary traditions, the state celebrates its cultural variety. Santa Fe has a thriving arts culture, with galleries, museums, and art festivals showing Native American art, Spanish colonial art, and contemporary works.

The cuisine of New Mexico reflects the state's varied background, with flavors influenced by Native American, Mexican, and Spanish traditions. The state is well-known for its use of chile peppers, both green and red, in a variety of recipes. Green and red chile sauces, enchiladas, tamales, and sopapillas are iconic New Mexican dishes.

The state is also well-known for its extensive musical tradition. Native American tribes have a long history of performing ceremonial and social music, which is frequently accompanied by drums, flutes, and singing. The guitar, violin, and other string instruments were brought to the region by Spanish and Mexican influences, resulting in the formation of new Mexican music genres such as rancheras, corridos, and mariachi.

Traditional dances, rituals, and crafts add to New Mexico's cultural fabric. Native American dances, such as the hypnotic hoop dance and the vivacious powwows, are essential components of tribal rites and festivities. Spanish and Mexican traditions, such as flamenco dance and folkloric performances, enrich the state's cultural fabric.

Historical sites and markers are located throughout New Mexico to preserve and remember the state's rich past. The San Miguel Mission in Santa Fe is considered the oldest church structure in the United States; the Palace of the Governors, which has served as a seat of government for centuries; and the Gila Cliff Dwellings, ancient cliff dwellings that offer a glimpse into the lives of the region's early inhabitants, are among the notable sites.

The history and culture of New Mexico are treasured and embraced by its citizens, who are proud of their rich background. The state's multicultural influences, artistic expressions, and historical landmarks make it an enthralling destination for anyone looking to learn more about the Land of Enchantment.

C. The inhabitants of New Mexico and their way of life

New Mexico's people are as diverse as the state's landscapes and cultures. Native Americans, Hispanics, Anglo-Americans, and other ethnic groups make up the population, each contributing to the fabric of New Mexico's society. Let's look at the manner of life and some remarkable characteristics of the inhabitants of New Mexico:

Cultural Diversity: New Mexico is noted for its varied heritage, which its citizens accept and cherish. Navajo, Apache, Pueblo, and other Native American tribes have a substantial presence in the state, preserving their ancient languages, customs, and art forms. The Hispanic and Latino community, with deep roots in Spanish and Mexican history, contributes to the state's cultural richness. Anglo-Americans and individuals of other ethnicities also contribute to the state's diversity.

Warm Hospitality: New Mexicans are known for being friendly and hospitable. Hospitality is profoundly embedded in the culture of the state, with residents frequently going out of their way to make guests feel welcome. Sharing traditional meals, providing advice on local sites, and engaging in polite conversations are all examples of hospitality.

Festivals and Traditions: Throughout the year, New Mexico organizes several festivals and cultural events. Native American dances, Hispanic fiestas,

Spanish religious processions, and art festivals are among the festivities that highlight the state's unique traditions. The Albuquerque International Balloon Fiesta, the Indian Market in Santa Fe, and several Pueblo feast days are all noteworthy events.

Art & Crafts: New Mexico boasts a vibrant arts sector that draws artists from all over the world. Traditional Native American pottery, jewelry, and textiles, as well as Spanish-influenced crafts like tinwork and woodcarving, reflect the state's artistic legacy. Many localities feature art galleries, studios, and workshops where visitors can get a firsthand look at the creative process.

Nature Connection: Many New Mexicans have a strong connection to the natural environment. Outdoor activities such as hiking, skiing, camping, and wildlife watching are available in the state's diverse landscapes, which include mountains, deserts, and forests. Many individuals have a profound respect for the state's natural beauty and regularly participate in outdoor activities.

Rural and Urban Living: Rural and urban living coexist in New Mexico, with small communities and larger cities coexisting. Rural communities are frequently close-knit, stressing community values and traditions. Cultural attractions, modern comforts, and a dynamic arts scene coexist in urban places such as Albuquerque and Santa Fe.

Strong Sense of Heritage: New Mexicans are proud of their history and heritage. The varied cultural influences of the state are visible in everyday life, from architecture and cuisine to celebrations and traditions. Through organizations, museums, and community activities, many residents actively participate in maintaining and promoting their cultural traditions.

New Mexico's way of life is a perfect blend of ethnic traditions, friendly hospitality, and a strong respect for the natural environment. The people of New Mexico exemplify the essence of the Land of Enchantment, cherishing their different backgrounds and appreciating the state's unique tapestry of cultures.

D. Language and communication

English is the most widely spoken language in New Mexico, and it is the primary language for business, education, and everyday communication. English-speaking residents can be found throughout the state, particularly in urban areas and popular tourist destinations.

Because of the state's historical ties with Spain and Mexico, Spanish has a significant presence in New Mexico. Many residents, particularly those of Hispanic descent, speak Spanish as a first or second language. Bilingual signs and Spanish are spoken more frequently in areas such as Santa Fe and northern New Mexico.

There are 23 Native American tribes in New Mexico, each with its own culture and language. Within their respective communities, Native American languages such as Navajo, Apache, Keres, Tewa, and others are spoken. While English is the most commonly used language for intercultural communication, opportunities to learn about and hear Native American languages may arise in specific cultural contexts.

Many people in New Mexico are bilingual, speaking both English and Spanish or English and a Native American language. This linguistic diversity adds to the state's cultural richness and allows for cross-cultural exchanges.

While English is widely spoken, knowing a few basic Spanish phrases can be beneficial and demonstrate respect for the local culture. Simple greetings, expressions of gratitude, and requests for directions are useful phrases to learn that can improve interactions with Spanish-speaking people.

It is critical to respect local languages and cultural diversity. Taking an interest in New Mexico's languages and cultures can help you make new friends and enrich your travel experiences in the state.

Visitors can gain a better understanding of New Mexico's heritage and connect with the communities that make the state truly
unique by embracing the state's linguistic and cultural diversity.

Chapter 1: Planning Your Trip to new mexico

A. Best Time to Visit New Mexico

The best time to visit New Mexico depends on your preferences and the activities in which you intend to participate. Here's a rundown of the seasons and what they have to offer:

Spring (March to May): Spring in New Mexico delivers warm temperatures and gorgeous scenery. The weather is often pleasant, with blossoming flowers and vegetation. It's an excellent season for outdoor activities such as hiking, exploring national parks, and visiting botanical gardens. Keep in mind that spring can be windy, especially in the afternoons.

Summer (June to August): Summers in New Mexico can be hot, especially in the southern and desert regions. Temperatures frequently surpass 90°F (32°C), however, higher elevations in the mountains provide some reprieve with milder temperatures. Summer is a fantastic time for outdoor excursions such as river rafting, camping, and exploring the high country if you can take the heat. The iconic Albuquerque International Balloon Fiesta, which is also a popular summer event, is held in early October.

Fall (September to November): Fall is a beautiful time to visit New Mexico, with cooler temperatures and the changing colors of the autumn foliage. September and October are particularly lovely, with good weather for outdoor activities and sightseeing. It's a perfect time to explore stunning landscapes, tour wineries, attend cultural festivals, and observe traditional harvest celebrations.

Winter (December to February): Winters in New Mexico vary based on geography.

Mountainous areas endure chilly temperatures and precipitation, making it a perfect period for winter sports such as skiing and snowboarding. The desert regions, such as Albuquerque and Santa Fe, have milder winters, but temperatures can drop below freezing at night. Winter is a slower season for tourism, allowing you to explore attractions and cultural places with fewer crowds.

Keep in mind that the elevation differences in New Mexico cause major temperature fluctuations between day and night throughout the year. It's always a good idea to check the weather prediction for your specific trip and pack appropriately.

It's also a good idea to think about any unique events or festivals you might wish to attend during your visit. Festivals such as the Santa Fe Indian Market, the Albuquerque International Balloon Fiesta, and different artistic and cultural events are conducted throughout the year and can enhance your New Mexico experience.

Overall, spring and fall are popular times to visit New Mexico due to the moderate weather and variety of outdoor activities and cultural events. However, each season has its own allure, and the best time to come ultimately depends on your interests, the activities you intend to partake in, and the experiences you desire.

B. Entry Requirements and Travel Tips

You must meet specific visa and entrance requirements to enter the United States, including New Mexico. The following is a summary of the general requirements:

Visa Waiver Program (VWP): Under the Visa Waiver Program, citizens of specified countries may be eligible to travel to the United States. This program provides you visa-free access to the country for up to 90 days for tourism or business. Before their trip, VWP travelers must apply for and receive authorization through the Electronic System for Travel Authorization (ESTA).

Non-Visa Waiver Program Countries: If you are not a citizen of a Visa Waiver Program nation, you must apply for a nonimmigrant visa at a U.S. embassy or consulate in your home country before visiting the United States. The sort of visa you require will be determined by the purpose of your travel, which could be a tourist (B-2) visa, a business (B-1) visa, or another relevant category.

Passport Validity: Make sure your passport is valid for at least six months beyond your planned stay in the United States. It is critical to research the passport validity criteria for your country of citizenship.

extra documents: Depending on your travel conditions, you may be required to produce extra documents such as a return ticket, proof of lodging, a travel itinerary, and proof of adequate finances to cover your expenses during your stay.

Customs and Border Protection (CBP) Procedure: When you arrive in the United States, you will be subjected to the Customs and Border Protection (CBP) procedure. This comprises your passport, visa (if applicable), and a completed arrival/departure form (typically Form I-94 or an electronic equivalent). CBP officials may interview you about the reason for your visit and the length of your stay.

It is important to note that entry requirements and visa regulations are subject to change, so it is critical to consult with the nearest U.S. embassy or consulate in your home country for the most up-to-date and accurate information regarding visa and entry requirements specific to your nationality.

Furthermore, due to the continuing COVID-19 epidemic, extra entrance criteria and travel restrictions may be in place. It is critical to stay up to speed on the newest COVID-19 travel advisories, health protocols, and entry requirements by visiting the official websites of the United States Department of State and the Centers for Disease Control and Prevention (CDC).

C. Transportation Options

New Mexico offers several transportation options to help you get around the state and explore its diverse attractions. Here are some common transportation options:

Car Rental:

Car rentals are a popular and convenient mode of transportation for exploring New Mexico. Here is some information and advice on car hire in the state:

Rental companies: Hertz, Avis, Budget, Enterprise, and National are among the well-known vehicle rental firms in New Mexico. These businesses have locations in major airports, such as the Albuquerque International Sunport, as well as in cities such as Albuquerque and Santa Fe.

Reservation: It is best to book a car rental in advance, especially during high travel seasons or if you have specific vehicle preferences. This guarantees availability and, in many cases, allows you to compare costs and locate the best discounts.

Requirements: To hire an automobile in New Mexico, you must normally meet the following requirements:

Valid Driver's License: You must have a valid driver's license from your home country or an International Driving Permit (IDP) to enter the United States. The minimum age to rent a car varies by rental company, although it is usually 21 or older. Drivers under the age of 25 may face additional regulations or costs from some firms.

Credit Card: For payment and as a security deposit, a major credit card in the renter's name is normally required.

Insurance: Additional insurance coverage choices, such as collision damage waivers or liability coverage, are frequently provided by car rental businesses. It is recommended that you check your current insurance policy and determine whether you require additional coverage.

Vehicle Options: Car rental businesses provide a variety of vehicle options, including economy vehicles, sedans, SUVs, and minivans. When choosing a vehicle, consider the number of people, luggage space, and the sort of terrain you intend to drive on.

Driving in New Mexico: Learn the local traffic rules and regulations in New Mexico. Follow speed restrictions, use a seat belt, and avoid using handheld gadgets while driving. When traveling in rural areas, be cautious because some roads may be unpaved or poorly maintained.

Fuel: Before you start your travel, make sure you understand the rental company's fuel policies. Some firms require you to return the vehicle with a full tank of gas, while others may allow you to purchase a full tank in advance and return it empty.

GPS and Maps: For navigating on your New Mexico road trip, consider renting a GPS navigation device or using a smartphone app. Having access to accurate instructions and maps will assist you in navigating the state's roadways and arriving at your preferred destinations.

Parking: Most New Mexico cities, including Albuquerque and Santa Fe, provide parking facilities, including metered street parking and parking garages. When visiting major tourist areas, be mindful of parking limits and taxes and plan appropriately.

Roadside help: inquire about the rental company's roadside help services. Knowing how to seek help in the event of an emergency or car malfunction might offer you peace of mind during your vacation.

Remember to inspect the rental car before driving away, noting any pre-existing damage and reporting it to the rental company as soon as possible. Following traffic laws, driving properly, and following the rental agreement will result in a pleasant and enjoyable automobile rental experience in New Mexico.

Public Transportation:

Public transportation in New Mexico, particularly in urban areas, provides convenient alternatives to driving. Here's a rundown of the state's public transportation options:

Services for buses:

ABQ RIDE (Albuquerque): The city of Albuquerque has a large bus system that services the city and its neighboring areas. ABQ RIDE has a variety of routes and schedules that cover important attractions, residential regions, and business districts.

Santa Fe Trails (Santa Fe): Santa Fe Trails is the city's public transportation system. The buses go between different neighborhoods, attractions, and the Santa Fe Plaza.

Rail Runner Express (Rail Runner):

The Rail Runner Express is a commuter train that runs between Santa Fe and Albuquerque, making several stops along the way. It is a convenient way to commute between the two cities and connects to other transit hubs.
Regional and intercity bus services are available.

New Mexico Park and Ride: The New Mexico Park and Ride service provides intercity bus services connecting locations around the state. These routes are very handy for travelling between big metropolitan areas.
Greyhound: Greyhound, a national bus company, operates in New Mexico, linking major cities and towns within the state as well as connecting to neighboring states.
Transportation Services:

Ride-sharing services such as Uber and Lyft are available in New Mexico, particularly in urban regions such as Albuquerque and Santa Fe. These services offer convenient transportation and may be accessible via smartphone apps.

It is crucial to note that public transit alternatives may differ based on your location and the time of day. It is best to examine the schedules, routes, and fees of the various transit options ahead of time.

Transit websites and smartphone applications, such as those operated by ABQ RIDE or Santa Fe Trails, can provide up-to-date information on routes, schedules, and fares.

Public transportation alternatives for long-distance travel inside the state may be restricted. In such instances, hiring a car or using intercity bus services such as Greyhound may be preferable.

Overall, New Mexico public transit can be a convenient and cost-effective way to explore urban regions, commute between cities, and lessen dependency on private vehicles.

Train:
New Mexico train travel is a picturesque and leisurely way to explore the state. The following are the main train options:

Southwest Chief, Amtrak:

The Southwest Chief is an Amtrak train route that goes from Chicago, Illinois, to Los Angeles, California, with stops in New Mexico. New Mexico's major stops include Raton, Las Vegas, Lamy (near Santa Fe), and Albuquerque.

The Southwest Chief offers a luxurious and relaxed travel experience, allowing passengers to take in the stunning scenery of New Mexico along the way.

The Southwest Chief's amenities may include comfortable seating, sleeping accommodations (such as roomettes and bedrooms), a dining car, a lounge car, and Wi-Fi (availability varies).

Rail Runner Express in New Mexico:

The New Mexico Rail Runner Express, while not a typical scenic rail route, is a commuter train service that runs between Santa Fe and Belen, with many stops along the way, including Albuquerque.

The Rail Runner Express provides a convenient mode of transit between these cities as well as connections to other transportation hubs such as the Albuquerque International Sunport.

The railway cars are spacious and well-equipped, with amenities like air conditioning, bathrooms, and bike racks.

Consider the following while arranging a rail trip in New Mexico:

Reservations: It is best to book ahead of time, especially during high travel seasons or if you have specific travel dates and preferences.

Check the rail schedules and plan your journey appropriately. Be mindful of any layovers or transfers, as well as the departure and arrival timings.

Purchasing tickets in advance is possible via the Amtrak website or at designated ticket counters. Before boarding the train, make sure you have your tickets handy.

Baggage: Research the baggage policies of the railway service you intend to use. Keep in mind any size or weight restrictions, and make sure your luggage is correctly tagged.

Amenities: Dining selections, Wi-Fi, power outlets, and sleeper rooms may differ depending on the train service and class of service. Check to see what amenities are available on the train route you intend to take.

Train travel can be a relaxing and pleasurable way to explore New Mexico's surroundings. Exploring the rail alternatives can add a new depth to your travel experience in the state, whether you're seeking a picturesque vacation or a handy transportation option between cities.

Air Travel:

Air travel is a popular and convenient way to get to and from New Mexico. The state contains many airports that handle both domestic and international flights. Here is some information regarding flying in New Mexico:

Albuquerque International Sunport (ABQ): Albuquerque International Sunport is New Mexico's largest and busiest airport. It is situated in Albuquerque, the state's capital. ABQ has a diverse range of domestic flights to major cities throughout the United States, as well as some international flights to Mexico.

Santa Fe Regional Airport (SAF) is located around 10 miles southwest of downtown Santa Fe. It mostly provides regional service to and from a few large centers, including Denver and Dallas. This airport serves as a convenient choice for visitors to Santa Fe and the neighboring areas.

Other Airports: Several other airports in New Mexico serve regional and smaller-scale aviation travel. These airports include Las Cruces International Airport (LRU), Roswell International Air Center (ROW), and Farmington's Four Corners Regional Airport

(FMN). These airports handle domestic flights and provide connections to major hubs.

Airlines: Several major airlines, including but not limited to Southwest Airlines, American Airlines, Delta Air Lines, United Airlines, and Alaska Airlines, provide flights to and from New Mexico's airports. Smaller regional airlines may also offer flights to specific locations within the state.

Domestic and International Flights: While the majority of flights to and from New Mexico are domestic, there are some international flights accessible. The Albuquerque foreign Sunport has a small number of foreign flights, mostly to Mexico. Connecting flights through major U.S. hubs is frequently the most convenient alternative for international tourists.

Ground Transportation: Ground transportation is offered at airports to assist you in reaching your final destination. Taxis, ride-sharing services, shuttles, and car rental firms are common examples of these possibilities. To guarantee a smooth transition from the airport to your target location, it is best to research and organize your ground transportation ahead of time.

Consider the airport that best meets your needs and the destinations you intend to visit when arranging your vacation to New Mexico. Check flight availability, compare pricing, and think about things like travel times, connections, and ground transportation choices.

It should be noted that flight timetables, airline options, and itineraries are subject to change. Always check with the airlines and airports for the most up-to-date information on flights, baggage allowances, security processes, and any travel advisories or COVID-19-related regulations.

Taxis and Ride-Sharing Services:

Taxis and ride-sharing services are convenient modes of transportation in New Mexico, especially in urban areas. Here is some information regarding the state's taxis and ride-sharing services:

Taxis:

Taxis are available in most major cities and villages in New Mexico, including Albuquerque, Santa Fe, and Las Cruces.

Taxis are usually available at authorized taxi stands, outside hotels, or by dialing a local taxi company.

Taxis in New Mexico are usually metered, with charges dependent on distance traveled and waiting time.

Taxi drivers are typically tipped between 10% and 15% of the fare.

Transportation Sharing Services (Uber, Lyft):

Uber and Lyft operate in several New Mexico cities and towns, including Albuquerque, Santa Fe, and Las Cruces.

These services are available via smartphone apps that allow you to request a trip, track the driver's arrival, and make cashless payments.

Uber and Lyft provide a variety of vehicle options, including basic automobiles, larger vehicles for groups, and luxury or high-end vehicles.

Fares for ride-sharing services are normally calculated based on distance and time, and they may change based on demand and other variables.

Aside from convenience, ride-sharing services frequently include features such as driver ratings, anticipated prices, and the opportunity to share your trip details with others for increased security.

Consider the following tips while using taxis or ride-sharing services in New Mexico:

Safety: Always ride in a licensed and trustworthy taxi or ride-sharing car. Check the driver's identification and that the car matches the information provided in the app or by the taxi operator.

Taxis often accept cash and credit cards, although ride-sharing services such as Uber and Lyft typically require a credit card linked to your account. It's usually a good idea to keep some cash on hand in case of card payment complications.

Taxis are normally available all day, however, ride-sharing services may have peak hours or periods of high demand. During peak periods, ride availability may be limited, and fares may be subject to surge pricing.

Ratings and Reviews: Make use of the rating and review system for taxis as well as ride-sharing services. Before requesting a ride, check the driver's ratings and reviews to ensure a great encounter.

Accessibility: If you have specific accessibility requirements, such as wheelchair-accessible vehicles, contact the taxi company or utilize the ride-sharing app's accessibility features to request appropriate transportation.

Remember to obey local traffic regulations, wear your seatbelt, and adhere to any additional instructions offered by the taxi or ride-sharing service. Always plan ahead of time, allow extra time for unexpected delays, and keep your items secure when using these services.

Guided Tours:
New Mexico guided tours provide an organized and educational method to discover the state's

attractions, history, and culture. There are numerous guided tour alternatives available, depending on whether you are interested in nature, history, art, or gastronomic experiences. Here's a rundown of the various sorts of guided tours available in New Mexico:

Tours of Cultural and Historical Interest:

Native American Pueblos: Many guided excursions focus on New Mexico's rich Native American culture and history. These tours frequently stop in historic Pueblo settlements like Acoma, Taos, and Zuni to learn about their traditions, architecture, and arts.

Santa Fe Historic District: Discover Santa Fe's historic district, which includes Adobe architecture, art galleries, and museums. Walking tours guide visitors through the city's history, including Spanish colonial and Native American influences.

Tours to historical places such as Chaco Canyon National Historical Park, Bandelier National Monument, and the Gila Cliff Dwellings are offered, where you may learn about past civilizations and their archaeological remains.

Nature and outdoor tours:

Balloon Rides: Take a hot air balloon flight to see New Mexico's stunning scenery from above. Albuquerque, in particular, is well-known for its annual International Balloon Fiesta and provides balloon rides all year.

National Parks and Monuments: Guided tours of New Mexico's national parks and monuments, such as Carlsbad Caverns National Park, White Sands National Monument, and Petroglyph National

Monument, are offered. These trips frequently contain instructional information about the region's geology, vegetation, and animals.

Hiking and Jeep trips: For outdoor activities, explore guided hiking trips or jeep tours in regions such as the Sandia Mountains, Rio Grande Gorge, or Taos Ski Valley. These tours offer magnificent vistas, wildlife viewing, and exploration of the region's natural beauties.

Tours of Art and Cuisine:

Santa Fe Art Tours: Take a guided tour of Santa Fe's thriving art scene, stopping at galleries, museums, and artist studios. You can learn about many art genres, such as traditional Native American art, modern works, and creations influenced by the Southwest.

Food and Wine Tours: Take guided food and wine tours to discover the flavors of New Mexico. These trips frequently include stops at local restaurants, food markets, and wineries, where guests can sample regional cuisines, traditional cuisine, and New Mexican wines.

Tours of the City and Architecture:

Trolley Tours in Albuquerque: Take a guided trolley tour across the city of Albuquerque. These excursions include the city's history, architecture, and noteworthy landmarks.

Historic Route 66: Take a guided tour of the famed Route 66, which runs through several New Mexico cities. These trips immerse you in the nostalgia of this renowned roadway by taking you to roadside sights, classic diners, and historic landmarks.

Consider the following when arranging guided tours in New Mexico:

Look for reliable trip companies and study feedback from prior participants.
Examine the tour's duration, inclusions, and any additional expenses.

Confirm whether transportation, food, or attraction admission prices are included.
Consider the tour's group size and if it offers a personalized and private experience or a larger group environment.
Check to see if the trip is offered in the language of your choice.
Take note of any safety warnings and any tour-specific requirements, such as required dress or physical fitness levels.

You can benefit from the knowledge and expertise of experienced guides by attending guided tours, which can provide vital insights into New Mexico's history, culture, and natural wonders.

It's important to consider your transportation needs based on your travel plans, destinations, and personal preferences. New Mexico's vast landscapes and attractions can require some driving and logistics, so it's advisable to plan ahead and select the transportation option that best suits your itinerary and comfort level.

D. Accommodation Choices

When it comes to accommodation choices in New Mexico, you'll find a variety of options to suit different preferences and budgets. Here are some common types of accommodations and a suggestion for the best neighborhood to stay in each of the major cities:

Hotels and Resorts:

Hotels and resorts are widely available throughout New Mexico, ranging from budget-friendly options to luxury accommodations. You'll find well-known hotel chains as well as unique boutique hotels and upscale resorts.

Best Neighborhood to Stay in Albuquerque: Downtown Albuquerque is a popular choice for its central location, proximity to attractions like Old Town, and a variety of hotels to suit different budgets.

Bed and Breakfasts:

New Mexico is known for its charming bed and breakfast establishments. These accommodations offer a more intimate and personalized experience, often with unique architectural features and homemade breakfasts.

Best Neighborhood to Stay in Santa Fe: The Historic District of Santa Fe is an excellent choice for bed and breakfast accommodations. This area is known for its adobe-style architecture, art galleries, and proximity to the Santa Fe Plaza.

Vacation Rentals:

Vacation rentals, such as apartments, condos, and houses, can be a great option for those seeking more space and flexibility during their stay. Websites like Airbnb and VRBO offer a wide range of vacation rental options across the state.

Best Neighborhood to Stay in Taos: The Taos Ski Valley area is a popular choice for vacation rentals, especially during the winter season. It offers easy access to skiing and outdoor activities.

Guest Ranches:

New Mexico's rich cowboy and ranching heritage make guest ranches a unique accommodation choice. These ranches provide an opportunity to experience the Western lifestyle and engage in activities like horseback riding and cattle drives.

Best Neighborhood to Stay in Ruidoso: The Ruidoso area, nestled in the mountains of southern New Mexico, offers guest ranches and a scenic environment for outdoor enthusiasts.

Campgrounds and RV Parks:

For those who enjoy camping and RV travel, New Mexico has numerous campgrounds and RV parks. These options allow you to immerse yourself in the state's natural beauty.

Best Neighborhood to Camp near Las Cruces: The Organ Mountains-Desert Peaks National

Monument, located just outside of Las Cruces, offers camping opportunities and stunning desert landscapes.

When choosing the best neighborhood to stay in, consider factors such as proximity to attractions, safety, convenience, and the ambiance you're seeking. It's also a good idea to research reviews, check the accessibility to public transportation or parking, and consider any specific requirements or preferences you may have.

Remember that availability and prices may vary depending on the season and local events, so it's advisable to book accommodations in advance, especially during peak travel periods.

Chapter 2: Exploring Major Cities

A. Albuquerque

Albuquerque, New Mexico's largest city, offers a distinct blend of history, culture, outdoor activities, and gastronomic delights. Old Town Albuquerque, located in the city's center, is one of the city's primary attractions. This historic quarter is filled with adobe structures, scenic plazas, shops, galleries, and restaurants. Visit the San Felipe de Neri Church, one of the city's oldest remaining structures, and the Plaza, where local artisans offer jewelry, ceramics, and other crafts. The Albuquerque Museum of Art and History, located in Old Town, exhibits the region's history and art.

The Petroglyph National Monument is a must-see for nature lovers. This national monument protects a large collection of Native American rock art. Hiking routes allow visitors to get up close and personal with the petroglyphs. The monument's Boca Negra Canyon area includes many short walks with interpretive markers describing the significance of the rock art.

Visitors can take a beautiful tram ride on the Sandia Peak Tramway to see stunning views of the city and neighboring regions. It ascends to the top of the Sandia Mountains as one of the world's longest aerial tramways. In the Cibola National Forest, the mountains also offer chances for outdoor activities such as hiking, mountain biking, and skiing (during the winter season).

Another famous destination is the Albuquerque BioPark, which includes the ABQ BioPark Zoo, Botanic Garden, Aquarium, and Tingley Beach. Visitors can explore the zoo's various species, wander through the Botanic Garden's stunning plants, discover aquatic life at the Aquarium, and enjoy fishing or boating at Tingley Beach.

The Indian Pueblo Cultural Center is a great place to learn about the rich Native American heritage and culture of New Mexico's 19 Pueblo villages. Exhibits, traditional dances, art galleries, and a café serving Native American food are available at the center.

The city of Albuquerque is also renowned as the "Hot Air Balloon Capital of the World." Several firms provide hot air balloon trips with spectacular views of the city and its surroundings, allowing visitors to experience the thrill of hot air ballooning. The Albuquerque International Balloon Fiesta is a must-see event if you visit in October. This important balloon festival offers hundreds of multicolored balloons in flight, as well as a variety of events and activities.

Foodies will enjoy visiting the city's rich culinary scene. Green chile stew, enchiladas, tamales, and sopapillas are among the foods popular in Albuquerque's New Mexican cuisine. There are various restaurants, ranging from casual to sophisticated, where guests can enjoy these cuisines.

Albuquerque also has festivals, art galleries, museums, and a dynamic downtown district with shops, restaurants, and entertainment venues. Visitors can learn about the local culture, participate in outdoor activities, and discover the distinctive attractions that make Albuquerque a remarkable visit.

B. Santa Fe

Santa Fe, New Mexico's capital, is well-known for its artistic and cultural legacy. Santa Fe emanates a distinct blend of Pueblo, Spanish, and Anglo influences, which may be seen in its architecture, gastronomy, and cultural scene. Visitors can enjoy a variety of sights and experiences in the city.

The Santa Fe Plaza, the city's heart, is a must-see sight in Santa Fe. The Plaza, which is surrounded by ancient buildings, is a center of activity with stores, galleries, and restaurants. The Palace of the Governors, which contains the New Mexico History Museum and highlights the state's rich history, is open to tourists. The Loretto Chapel, noted for its amazing stairway, is another iconic attraction.

Art lovers will find Santa Fe to be a creative haven. Canyon Road is a well-known roadway dotted with art galleries and studios displaying a wide range of artwork. Visitors to the lively art scene can immerse themselves in anything from traditional Native American art to contemporary marvels. The city also has prominent museums, such as the Georgia O'Keeffe Museum, which is dedicated to the work of the legendary American artist, and the Museum of International Folk Art, which exhibits folk art from around the world.

The architectural attractiveness of Santa Fe is reflected in its adobe buildings and distinct Santa Fe architecture. Visitors can explore the historic district, taking in the adobe structures and the city's distinct architectural personality. With its stunning stained glass windows and exquisite architecture, the Cathedral Basilica of St. Francis of Assisi is another architectural wonder.

Santa Fe's culinary scene is a joy for foodies. The city's cuisine is influenced by Native American and Spanish civilizations. Traditional New Mexican cuisine, such as green chile stew, enchiladas, and tamales, is available to visitors. Santa Fe also has upmarket restaurants, quiet cafes, and bustling farmers' markets where visitors can sample the local cuisine.

Throughout the year, Santa Fe organizes a range of cultural events. The city is well-known for its traditional Indian Market, which features Native American arts and crafts, as well as its Spanish Market, which features Spanish Colonial art. During the summer season, the Santa Fe Opera, nestled against the breathtaking backdrop of the Sangre de Cristo Mountains, delivers world-class performances.

The city's rich cultural past is highlighted by its numerous festivals, music events, and historical sites. The Indian Pueblo Cultural Center allows visitors to learn about the history and traditions of Native American communities. The Santa Fe Fiesta, a multi-day celebration with parades, music, and dancing, is another way the city honors its legacy.

With its blend of art, culture, architecture, and gastronomic pleasures, Santa Fe provides a one-of-a-kind and engaging experience. Visitors may immerse themselves in the city's rich history, experience its lively art scene, savor delectable cuisine, and celebrate the numerous cultural traditions that make Santa Fe a truly unique destination.

C. Taos

Taos, in northern New Mexico, is a lovely town recognized for its artistic culture, natural beauty, and rich Native American heritage.

Taos is home to the Taos Pueblo, a UNESCO World Heritage Site and one of the United States' oldest continuously inhabited towns. Taos Pueblo's multi-story adobe houses have been inhabited by Native Americans for over a thousand years. Visitors can join guided tours to learn about the Taos Pueblo community's history, culture, and traditions.

Taos itself has a variety of activities and experiences to offer. Taos Plaza is the town's hub, with a central plaza surrounded by adobe structures that house stores, galleries, and restaurants. Visitors can stroll around the historic neighborhood, shop in one-of-a-kind boutiques, and discover local artwork and crafts.

The Rio Grande Gorge is a must-see for environment lovers. The Rio Grande River sculpted the impressive gorge, which provides stunning panoramas and hiking options. Visitors can walk across the Rio Grande Gorge Bridge, one of the highest bridges in the United States, to get a bird's-eye view of the gorge and its surroundings.

Taos is also well-known for its excellent skiing and outdoor activities. During the winter season, the Taos Ski Valley in the Sangre de Cristo Mountains provides superb skiing and snowboarding options.

During the summer, tourists can enjoy hiking, mountain biking, and river rafting amid the stunning alpine scenery.

The town has a vibrant arts sector that draws artists and craftspeople from all over the world. Taos Art Colony, founded in the early twentieth century, has been a center for artistic expression. Visitors can visit a variety of art galleries and studios that showcase a wide spectrum of artistic styles, from classic to contemporary.

Taos' cultural activities are quite important. Taos Pueblo Powwow is a lively celebration of Native American culture that includes traditional dances, music, and arts and crafts. Another famous event is the Taos Solar Music Festival, which combines live music performances with a focus on renewable energy.

Taos is well-known for its distinctive architecture, in addition to its cultural and outdoor amenities. The rich tones and distinctive style of the adobe houses add to the town's attractiveness. Visitors can tour the Kit Carson Home and Museum, which is dedicated to the famed frontiersman, and learn about the region's history.

Taos offers a unique combination of natural beauty, artistic expression, and cultural depth. Visitors can learn about Native American history, visit art galleries, participate in outdoor activities, and see the town's distinctive architectural style. Taos offers a riveting and rewarding experience for anyone, whether it's experiencing Taos Pueblo traditions, admiring the gorgeous vistas, or connecting with the local arts community.

Chapter 3: Natural Wonders and Outdoor Activities

A. Carlsbad Caverns National Park

Carlsbad Caverns National Park, in southeastern New Mexico, is a captivating underground wonderland that draws people from all over the world.

Carlsbad Caverns is a massive labyrinth of limestone caves, with over 119 caves reported to exist within the park. Carlsbad Cavern is the most well-known and accessible cave, featuring a succession of large underground chambers filled with spectacular stalactites, stalagmites, columns, and other distinctive rock formations. The cavern is a natural marvel built over millions of years by water erosion.

Visitors to Carlsbad Caverns can explore the cave on their own or with the assistance of a ranger. The Big Room Tour, which takes guests on a 1.25-mile circular track through the cavern's largest chamber, is the most popular. The paved and well-lit trail allows visitors to examine the intricate formations and learn about the geology, history, and environment of the cave.

Witnessing the bat flight is another one-of-a-kind event at Carlsbad Caverns. Thousands of Mexican free-tailed bats live in the cave from May to October and emerge in a magnificent mass exodus at sunset to feed. Visitors can see this magnificent scene from the outdoor amphitheater at the cave's entrance. It's important to note that bat flying is a natural occurrence that can be altered by weather and other variables, so it's best to check with the park for the most up-to-date information.

Carlsbad Caverns also offers wild cave tours, which allow guests to explore undeveloped areas of the cave with a guide. Crawling, climbing, and navigating through small channels are all part of these trips, which provide a thrilling and immersive experience for anyone looking for a deeper investigation of the caves.

Carlsbad Caverns National Park has scenic hiking routes and various desert landscapes above ground. The park covers a wide section of the Chihuahuan Desert, and visitors can enjoy the desert flora and animals as well as panoramic views of the surrounding mountains on leisurely walks or more difficult climbs.

The park offers a visitor center where visitors may learn about the cave system, its geological features, and the unique environment that it supports. In addition, the visitor center has a gift shop and a cafeteria where guests can have refreshments.

Carlsbad Caverns National Park provides a really breathtaking experience, allowing visitors to explore the incredible underground world and admire nature's beauties. Carlsbad Caverns is a must-see site for nature enthusiasts, adventure seekers, and anybody captivated by the mysteries beneath the Earth's surface, from the beautiful formations in the caverns to the fascinating bat flight and the picturesque splendor of the surrounding desert.

B. White Sands National Park

White Sands National Park, in southern New Mexico, is a one-of-a-kind and breathtaking natural phenomenon.

The huge expanse of sparkling white gypsum sand dunes at White Sands National Park creates a bizarre and otherworldly landscape. The park is about 275 square miles in size, making it the world's largest gypsum dune field. Over thousands of years, gypsum crystals eroded from adjacent mountains and accumulated in the Tularosa Basin, forming the dunes.

White Sands visitors can experience the dunes through a number of activities. One of the most popular activities is simply walking or hiking on the soft, cool beaches. The park has a number of approved routes of varied lengths and difficulty that allow visitors to experience the unusual sensation of walking on white gypsum dunes. The Alkali Flat Trail, a five-mile circle that takes tourists deep into the dune field, provides a more demanding and secluded experience.

Another popular activity at White Sands is sledding down the dunes. Visitors can rent or buy plastic sleds from the tourist center and slide down the dunes' steep slopes, offering both children and adults a thrilling and memorable experience.

Sandboarding is another popular activity, with some visitors bringing their own boards to ride the dunes.

Photographers will discover White Sands to be a photographer's dream location. The interplay of light and shadow on the white sand, particularly at sunrise and sunset, creates a stunning atmosphere and provides numerous shooting opportunities.

The park offers ranger-led programs and guided tours that educate visitors about the area's unique environment, geology, and cultural history. Interpretive presentations, guided hikes, and stargazing events may be included in these programs, helping visitors to develop a better knowledge and appreciation of the park's environmental and cultural significance.

Camping is permitted within the park, allowing visitors to spend the night under the starry desert sky. Reservations are essential, especially during high seasons, because the park includes designated camping areas with basic facilities.

It's vital to note that the park's severe desert environment can be difficult to navigate, especially during the summer months when temperatures can soar. To stay hydrated, visitors should pack sunscreen, hats, and plenty of water. Sandstorms are also possible, so keep an eye on the park's website or visitor center for any weather-related cautions or closures.

White Sands National Park provides a completely unique and awe-inspiring experience for tourists, allowing them to immerse themselves in the majesty of the white gypsum dune.

C. The Chaco Culture National Historical Park

The Chaco Culture National Historical Park is a UNESCO World Heritage Site that preserves the ruins of an indigenous Puebloan culture that flourished in the region from around 850 to 1250 AD. The park, which spans over 34,000 acres, is known for its extraordinary architectural and celestial alignments.

The Chaco Canyon, a lonely and magnificent canyon setting that was once a center of ancient Puebloan culture, is at the heart of Chaco Culture National Historical Park. The canyon contains several gigantic stone structures known as great houses, which served as ceremonial and administrative centers for the original Puebloans. Pueblo Bonito, the largest and most recognizable great house, is a massive complex with about 600 rooms.

Visitors to Chaco Culture National Historical Park can take self-guided tours or participate in ranger-led programs to view the ruins of the great dwellings. The park has a network of pathways that allow visitors to stroll amid the ancient structures, giving them a sense of the architecture's grandeur and complexity. The Pueblo Alto Loop Trail and the Pueblo del Arroyo Trail are popular options that lead to a variety of beautiful home locations.

Chaco Canyon also has several interesting astronomical features. The canyon's houses and constructions are coordinated with astronomical occurrences like solstices and equinoxes, demonstrating the original Puebloans' excellent grasp of astronomy. The Sun Dagger location, for example, has a one-of-a-kind rock carving that forms a pattern of light and shadow during certain times of the year.

Chaco Culture National Historical Park, in addition to archaeological sites, provides possibilities for stargazing, hiking, and camping. The park's night skies are particularly black and clear, making it an excellent place for seeing celestial wonders. The canyon is traversed by several hiking paths, allowing visitors to explore the varied landscapes and appreciate the natural beauty of the area. The Gallo Campground offers minimal facilities and a peaceful area for camping.

The Chaco Culture National Historical Park visitor center provides information on the site's history, culture, and significance. Exhibits and informative displays provide information about the indigenous Puebloan people and their relationship with the land. Ranger-led events, such as guided walks and talks, offer additional chances to learn about the park's archaeological findings and cultural history.

Because of its isolated position, Chaco Culture National Historical Park may only be reached by unpaved roads. It's a good idea to check road conditions and plan ahead of time, especially during bad weather. Visitors should also bring enough drink, food, and clothing, as services and amenities are restricted within the area.

Chaco Culture National Historical Park takes tourists on a fascinating journey into the ancient past, allowing them to immerse themselves in the rich history and architectural wonders of the indigenous Puebloan culture. Its huge ruins, astronomical alignments, and distant beauty make it a genuinely unique and awe-inspiring location for archaeology, Native American history, and cultural research.

D. Gila National Forest

Gila National Forest, in southwestern New Mexico, is a vast and diverse wilderness area with beautiful vistas, outdoor recreation options, and a rich ecological history.

Gila National Forest, with over 3.3 million acres of mountains, canyons, woods, and rivers, is one of the largest national forests in the United States. The forest is named after the Gila River, which runs through it, and it contains a diverse range of ecosystems, including high mountain summits, deep valleys, and vast forests.

The woodland is well-known for its picturesque and rough beauty. It is home to the Gila Wilderness, the country's first designated wilderness area, which covers around 558,014 acres. The Gila Wilderness is famous for its stunning vistas, inaccessible terrain, and plentiful animals. It provides many chances for backpacking, hiking, camping, and animal viewing. The varied trails that run through the countryside provide access to hidden waterfalls, historic cliff dwellings, and stunning vistas.

Outdoor aficionados will love the Gila National Forest. It is ideal for fishing, hunting, horseback riding, mountain biking, and off-road vehicle exploration. The forest is crisscrossed with a vast network of paths and forest roads that allow tourists to discover its picturesque delights and hidden secrets.

The Gila Cliff Dwellings National Monument is one of the attractions of the Gila National Forest. This archaeological site, located within the forest, features well-preserved cliff homes built by the ancient Mogollon people approximately 700 years ago. Visitors can enjoy a guided tour of the houses and learn about the Mogollon culture and history.

Wildlife abounds in Gila National Forest, and visitors may spot mule deer, elk, black bears, mountain lions, and a large diversity of bird species. The rare and endangered Mexican gray wolf also lives in the forest, and efforts are underway to reintroduce and safeguard this iconic animal.

Camping is a popular activity in Gila National Forest, which has a variety of constructed campgrounds as well as dispersed camping locations. The forest provides a variety of camping opportunities, ranging from campgrounds with facilities like restrooms and picnic tables to more rustic and secluded backcountry camping spots.

Visitors to the Gila National Forest should bring proper equipment, water, and supplies, as services and amenities may be restricted in some locations. For the most up-to-date information on road conditions, weather, and any specific regulations or limits, see the forest's official website or call the ranger district.

Gila National Forest provides a thrilling and immersive outdoor experience, allowing visitors to connect with nature, explore unspoiled wilderness areas, and appreciate southern New Mexico's various landscapes. Gila National Forest, with its rocky mountains, deep valleys, and rich wildlife, is a haven for outdoor enthusiasts and environment lovers looking for adventure, seclusion, and natural beauty.

E.   Outdoor   Adventures: Hiking, Camping, and Wildlife Viewing

Hiking, camping, and animal-viewing aficionados will find plenty of outdoor activities in New Mexico. Here are some popular outdoor adventure places and activities in the state:

Hiking in the Sangre de Cristo Mountains: Located in northern New Mexico, the Sangre de Cristo Mountains offer excellent hiking options. Trails such as Wheeler Mountain, New Mexico's highest mountain, and the Santa Fe Baldy provide breathtaking vistas of alpine landscapes, wildflowers, and animals.

Camping in the Carson National Forest: The Carson National Forest, which stretches throughout northern New Mexico, has several campgrounds and scattered camping possibilities. There are possibilities for all types of camping aficionados, from quiet sites along rivers and lakes to developed campgrounds with facilities.

Wildlife Viewing in the Bosque del Apache National Wildlife Refuge: Located in central New Mexico, the Bosque del Apache National Wildlife Refuge is an excellent location for birdwatching and wildlife viewing. During the winter, the refuge attracts thousands of migratory species, including sandhill cranes and snow geese.

Backpacking in the Gila Wilderness: Within the Gila National Forest, the Gila Wilderness is a backpacker's paradise. It provides a unique and remote wilderness experience with its rough landscapes, deep valleys, and hot springs. The Continental Divide Trail winds across the wilderness, providing chances for long-distance hiking.

Exploring the Organ Mountains-Desert Peaks National Monument: The Organ Mountains-Desert Peaks National Monument, located near Las Cruces in southern New Mexico, offers a variety of hiking paths with different desert vistas. The area is well-known for its unusual rock formations, archaeological sites, and chances to see wildlife such as bighorn sheep and reptiles.

Valle Vidal Wildlife Viewing: Located within the Carson National Forest, Valle Vidal is a magnificent mountain valley famed for its wildlife. While exploring the valley's paths and meadows, visitors may see elk, mule deer, black bears, and a variety of bird species.

Camping & Hiking in the White Mountains: The White Mountains, which are part of the Lincoln National Forest, provide spectacular camping and hiking options. The area is recognized for its cool mountain air, beautiful lakes, and thick forests, which provide a welcome respite during the scorching summer months.

Sandboarding at White Sands National Park: Visitors to White Sands National Park in southern New Mexico can enjoy the unique thrill of sandboarding. Rent a sandboard or sled from the visitor center for a thrilling ride down the vast white gypsum dunes.

To reduce your environmental impact when participating in outdoor activities in New Mexico, be prepared and follow Leave No Trace guidelines. Check the weather, pack adequate equipment, bring lots of water, and be informed of any unique restrictions or requirements for the location you intend to visit. It's also a good idea to tell someone about your plans and trek or camp with a buddy for safety.

Chapter 4: Cultural and Historical Sites

A. Acoma Pueblo

The Acoma Pueblo, popularly known as "Sky City," is a cultural and historical landmark in western New Mexico.

Acoma Pueblo is perched atop Acoma Sky City, a 367-foot-tall sandstone mesa. It is one of North America's oldest continuously inhabited communities, dating back over 1,000 years. The Acoma people live in the pueblo and have preserved their cultural traditions and way of life for generations.

A visit to Acoma Pueblo is a one-of-a-kind and immersive experience. The pueblo is accessible through guided tours offered by Acoma inhabitants who share insights into the Acoma people's history, culture, and daily life. You'll discover multi-story adobe buildings that have been painstakingly kept and maintained over the years as you explore the village.

The beautiful San Esteban del Rey Mission, a Spanish mission church built in the early 17th century, is one of the highlights of a visit to Acoma Pueblo. The mission is an amazing example of cultural interchange during the colonial period, with a blend of Spanish and Native American architectural styles.

Acoma Pueblo is well-known for its pottery, which is regarded as among the best in the Southwest. The Acoma people have a long tradition of manufacturing pottery, and you can watch the difficult process and buy stunning handcrafted pottery straight from the craftsmen.

During your stay, you will also be able to enjoy stunning panoramic views of the surrounding desert terrain. The mesa provides breathtaking views of the New Mexico landscape, highlighting the region's natural splendor.

It is crucial to note that Acoma Pueblo is a sacred site for the Acoma people, and visitors are asked to observe the community's customs and traditions. Certain sites may have photography limitations, so it's best to listen to your tour guide's advice.

Acoma Pueblo is situated around 60 miles west of Albuquerque. Reservations are required for guided tours, which are the most popular way to see the pueblo. The trips usually leave from the Sky City Cultural Center, which has a museum, an art gallery, and a gift store where you can learn about Acoma's history and culture.

A visit to Acoma Pueblo provides a once-in-a-lifetime opportunity to learn about the Acoma people's rich heritage and ongoing traditions. It gives tourists a better understanding of their history, artistry, and spiritual connection to the country.

B. Petroglyph National Monument

Petroglyph National Monument, located in Albuquerque, New Mexico, is a unique cultural and natural attraction.

The Petroglyph National Monument covers the huge West Mesa volcanic basalt escarpment. With over 25,000 petroglyphs identified to date, the monument has one of the highest concentrations of petroglyphs (rock carvings) in North America. Native American and Spanish cultures created these antique artworks between 400 and 700 years ago.

Petroglyph National Monument allows you to explore the rough scenery and learn about the region's rich cultural heritage. The monument has several hiking paths that lead to various petroglyph sites. The Boca Negra Canyon region is a popular starting place, with a paved trail that leads to a variety of petroglyphs engraved into volcanic rocks. Along the walk, interpretive signs explain the meaning and significance of the petroglyphs.

You'll be able to observe diverse petroglyph patterns portraying animals, humans, geometric shapes, and cultural symbols as you stroll across the monument. Each petroglyph tells a tale and offers insight into the lives and beliefs of the ancient people who lived in the area.

Petroglyph National Monument, in addition to the petroglyphs, provides breathtaking views of the surrounding desert terrain, including the Sandia Mountains to the east and the city of Albuquerque below. The monument is also home to a wide variety of plant and animal species, making it a perfect destination for nature lovers.

It is critical to respect the petroglyphs and the surrounding environment when visiting the Petroglyph National Monument. To guarantee the preservation of the petroglyphs for future generations, touching or climbing on them is banned. To help protect the site's natural and cultural integrity, stay on designated trails, carry out any trash you bring, and leave the area as you find it.

Petroglyph National Monument is located on Albuquerque's west side, conveniently accessible from the city center. The visitor center explains the monument's history, geology, and cultural significance. Rangers and volunteers are on hand to answer inquiries and recommend the finest routes to explore based on your interests and fitness level.

Petroglyph National Monument provides a unique opportunity to engage with the Southwest's rich cultural heritage and experience the magnificent rock carvings left behind by past civilizations. It's a destination of natural beauty and historical significance, where you can learn about the region's art and history.

C. El Santuario de Chimayó

The Santuario de Chimayó is a well-known pilgrimage destination in Chimayó, New Mexico. It is a revered spiritual site that draws visitors from all over the world. More information on El Santuario de Chimayó can be found here:

El Santuario de Chimayó is a modest adobe church with significant cultural and religious importance. It is well-known for its therapeutic reputation and is sometimes referred to as the "Lourdes of America." During Holy Week, when hundreds of pilgrims travel to seek blessings and healing, the sanctuary is especially respected.

El Santuario de Chimayó dates back to the early nineteenth century. A local friar discovered a crucifix buried on a small hill, that was thought to have magical abilities, according to mythology. The place became well-known for its therapeutic abilities as word spread. The current church was built in the late 1800s and serves as a tribute to the local community's faith and commitment.

The church is a small adobe structure with a lovely patio. Inside, there's a modest chapel with religious items, including the recently unearthed crucifix. Pilgrims' contributions, such as pictures, crutches, and scribbled prayers, decorate the walls.

One of the main draws of El Santuario de Chimayó is the "holy dirt." Pilgrims think the soil discovered in a small compartment within the cathedral has medicinal abilities. Visitors are urged to take a tiny amount of dirt with them to use for healing or to give to loved ones.

For many, the trip to El Santuario de Chimayó is a deeply spiritual experience. Pilgrims walk kilometers from various regions to reach the sanctuary. Some pilgrims go as an act of faith or penance, while others seek medical or spiritual recovery. During Holy Week, the atmosphere is especially lively, with processions, prayer vigils, and special religious events taking place.

Aside from its religious significance, the village of Chimayó is beautiful and well worth seeing. It is notable for its traditional weaving and the Rancho de Chimayó restaurant, which serves traditional New Mexican food.

Visiting El Santuario de Chimayó allows you to observe pilgrims' dedication and faith, as well as experience the spiritual aura of this precious spot. The sanctuary provides a profound and meaningful experience for those seeking healing, religious understanding, or cultural immersion.

D. New Mexico Museum of Art

The New Mexico Museum of Art is a well-known cultural institution in the city of Santa Fe, New Mexico. It is dedicated to preserving, presenting, and understanding New Mexico and Southwest art and culture. More information about the New Mexico Museum of Art may be found here:

The museum was founded in 1917 as the Art Gallery of the Museum of New Mexico and is the state's oldest art museum. It is housed in a historic Pueblo Revival-style edifice created by renowned architect Isaac Rapp that is regarded as a work of art in its own right.

The New Mexico Museum of Art houses a broad collection of artworks from many time periods, styles, and materials. Over 20,000 pieces, including paintings, sculptures, prints, photographs, and textiles, are part of the permanent collection. The collection focuses on artwork done in New Mexico or by artists influenced by the region.

Visitors can visit the museum's galleries and discover works by well-known painters such as Georgia O'Keeffe, Gustave Baumann, Marsden Hartley, and Fritz Scholder, among others. The collection features a mix of traditional and contemporary art, reflecting New Mexico's diverse artistic traditions and cultural diversity.

Aside from the permanent collection, the museum presents temporary exhibitions that focus on various subjects, artists, and art styles. These rotating exhibitions offer viewers new viewpoints as well as the opportunity to interact with new and thought-provoking artwork.

To enrich the visiting experience and encourage a greater knowledge and enjoyment of art, the museum also offers educational programs, workshops, lectures, and events. These programs cater to people of various ages and backgrounds, making art available to a wide range of people.

The New Mexico Museum of Art is a short walk from the historic Santa Fe Plaza in downtown Santa Fe. The surrounding area is densely packed with art galleries, boutiques, and restaurants, making it a perfect destination for art and culture fans.

Visiting the New Mexico Museum of Art is a once-in-a-lifetime opportunity to immerse yourself in New Mexico's lively art scene and get insights into the region's rich artistic heritage. Whether you are an art enthusiast or simply like cultural events, the museum takes you on a riveting trip through New Mexico's and beyond's artistic past.

E. Palace of the Governors

The Palace of the Governors is an iconic historical edifice in Santa Fe, New Mexico, located on the historic Santa Fe Plaza. It is one of the country's oldest continuously occupied public buildings and acts as a museum and emblem of the state's rich history.

The Palace of the Governors was built in the early 17th century to serve as the headquarters of the Spanish colonial government in Santa Fe. It has witnessed several historical events and transformations over the years, including periods of Spanish, Mexican, and American rule. The unusual adobe architecture of the structure represents the region's Spanish Colonial heritage.

The Palace of the Governors now houses the New Mexico History Museum, which celebrates the state's unique cultural heritage and history. The museum's exhibits cover a wide range of topics, including Native American presence, Spanish colonialism, the Mexican period, and American expansion.

The long gateway (covered walkway) along the building's façade, which serves as a gathering place for Native American craftsmen selling traditional goods such as jewelry, ceramics, and textiles, is one of the museum's highlights. Native American artists have been selling their goods at the Palace of the Governors for almost a century, adding to the site's cultural richness.

Explore the museum's galleries to learn about New Mexico's rich and complicated history via artifacts, photographs, documents, and interactive displays. The exhibitions include a variety of topics, including the Santa Fe Trail, the Atomic Age, the Civil War, and the varied groups that have defined the state.

The Palace Press, a working letterpress print studio adjacent to the Palace of the Governors, creates limited-edition books and other printed items. Visitors can learn about traditional bookmaking skills and see the printing process.

The Palace of the Governors also offers guided tours, which provide in-depth information on the building's history and significance. Knowledgeable advisors augment the visitor experience by sharing stories, anecdotes, and historical context.

The Palace of the Governors is not just a museum, but also a hub of cultural and social activity in Santa Fe. Throughout the year, it organizes a variety of events, lectures, and concerts, adding to the city's thriving arts and culture scene.

A visit to the Palace of the Governors provides an opportunity to travel back in time and obtain a better grasp of New Mexico's rich and diverse past. It is a must-see location for history buffs, art lovers, and anybody interested in learning about the region's cultural legacy.

F. Billy the Kid Trail

The Billy the Kid Trail in New Mexico is a historic trail that takes visitors on a journey through the lives and tales surrounding the iconic criminal, Billy the Kid.

The route includes various cities and landmarks related to Billy the Kid and offers insights into the Wild West era as well as the renowned figure himself. More information on the Billy the Kid Trail can be found here:

The Billy the Kid Trail traces the steps of the notorious bandit who rose to fame in the late 1800s. The path starts in Fort Sumner, a town in eastern New Mexico where Billy the Kid died tragically in 1881. Visitors to Fort Sumner can learn about the history and mythology surrounding his life by visiting the Billy the Kid Museum and the Old Fort Sumner Museum.

The road continues from Fort Sumner to Lincoln, a small hamlet at the epicenter of the Lincoln County War, a deadly struggle in which Billy the Kid played a key role. Lincoln's historic buildings, such as the Lincoln County Courthouse and the Tunstall Store, have been preserved, giving visitors a look into the Wild West era.

The town of White Oaks, which was a booming mining town during Billy the Kid's time, is next on the trail. Although much of the village has vanished over time, a few historic structures remain, including the No Scum Allowed Saloon, where Billy the Kid is claimed to have spent time.

The town of Silver City, located further up the path, has ties to Billy the Kid due to his involvement in the Lincoln County War. The Silver City Museum, which features exhibits on the region's history and the events surrounding Billy the Kid's life, is open to visitors.

Throughout the path, you'll come across historical markers, museums, and interpretive displays that present information about Billy the Kid's life and exploits. While the specific circumstances of Billy the Kid's life are veiled in myth and folklore, the route allows visitors to visit the locations linked to his outlaw notoriety.

The Billy the Kid Trail immerses visitors in the history of the Wild West and provides a deeper understanding of the life and legacy of one of

America's most legendary criminals. Whether you're a history buff, a follower of Western folklore, or simply curious about the time period, the Billy the Kid Trail offers an enthralling tour through New Mexico's landscapes and tales.

Chapter 5: Native American Heritage

A. Native American Tribes in New Mexico

New Mexico has a rich and diversified Native American heritage, with several tribes and Pueblos existing there. Here are some of New Mexico's Native American tribes and Pueblos:

The Navajo Nation is the largest Native American tribe in the United States, with a sizable population in New Mexico. The Navajo people, also known as the Diné, have their own language, culture, and art forms.

The Acoma Pueblo, often known as "Sky City," is one of North America's oldest continuously inhabited cities. It is perched above a mesa and provides a diverse cultural experience, including traditional ceramics and the arts.

The Zuni Pueblo is famous for its beautiful jewelry, pottery, and traditional dances. The Zuni people are noted for their spiritual beliefs and appreciation for nature, as well as their distinct language.

Taos Pueblo: The Taos Pueblo is a UNESCO World Heritage Site and one of the United States' oldest continuously inhabited villages. The Pueblo is well-known for its multi-story adobe structures and bustling arts and crafts scene.

Santa Clara Pueblo: Located near Espaola, Santa Clara Pueblo is famed for its pottery, particularly blackware, and redware. Traditional feast days and dances are also held at the pueblo and are available to the public.

Jemez Pueblo: Located in the Jemez Mountains, the Jemez Pueblo offers a unique cultural experience. Visitors can tour the Red Rocks and learn about Pueblo's history and traditions at the Walatowa Visitor Center.

Cochiti Pueblo: The Cochiti Pueblo is well-known for its ceramics, traditional dances, and the annual Cochiti Pueblo Feast Day, which features traditional ceremonies and celebrations.

Laguna Pueblo: Located west of Albuquerque, the Laguna Pueblo boasts a rich cultural legacy that includes pottery, jewelry, and traditional dances. The Pueblo is well-known for its annual Feast Day, which draws guests from all over.

These are only a few of New Mexico's Native American tribes and pueblos. Each tribe has its own history, traditions, and contributions to the cultural environment of the state. Exploring New Mexico's

Native American communities allows you to learn about their rich heritage, connect with craftspeople, and appreciate their continuing cultural legacy.

B. Cultural Centers and Museums

Several cultural institutes and museums in New Mexico promote and highlight the state's rich heritage and artistic traditions. Here are some of New Mexico's notable cultural centers and museums:

The Indian Pueblo Cultural Center (Albuquerque) is dedicated to conserving and promoting the history, art, and culture of New Mexico's 19 pueblos. It has exhibits, performances, workshops, and a museum store where you may buy Native American products and artwork.

The Museum of Indian Arts and Culture (Santa Fe) focuses on the art, history, and culture of Native

American tribes in New Mexico and elsewhere. It houses a large collection of Native American pottery, jewelry, textiles, and contemporary art, which provides insight into the various Native American cultures.

Wheelwright Museum of the American Indian (Santa Fe): The Wheelwright Museum features a diverse collection of Native American art, with a focus on the Southwest region. It includes textiles, jewelry, pottery, and paintings, as well as traditional and contemporary pieces.

The National Hispanic Cultural Center (Albuquerque) honors the heritage, art, and accomplishments of Hispanic and Latino populations in New Mexico and the greater Hispanic globe. Art exhibitions, live performances, film screenings, and cultural events are held here.

New Mexico Museum of Natural History and Science (Albuquerque): This museum investigates New Mexico's natural history, geology, and paleontology. It has interactive displays such as dinosaur fossils, a planetarium, and the DynaTheater.

Santa Fe's Georgia O'Keeffe Museum: This museum is dedicated to the life and work of renowned artist Georgia O'Keeffe, and it houses a large collection of her paintings, drawings, and sculptures. It reveals her artistic vision as well as her intimate affinity to New Mexico's landscapes.

Santa Fe Museum of International Folk Art: This museum houses one of the world's most substantial collections of international folk art. Textiles, ceramics, woodwork, and other traditional and contemporary art forms from various countries are featured.

The New Mexico History Museum (Santa Fe): Located next to the Palace of the Governors, the New Mexico History Museum covers New Mexico's history and cultural legacy. It has exhibits on a variety of subjects, such as the Spanish Colonial period, Native American history, and the Santa Fe Trail.

These cultural institutions and museums provide interesting and immersive experiences that allow visitors to learn about and appreciate New Mexico's many cultural traditions and artistic expressions. Whether you're interested in Native American heritage, Hispanic culture, or the state's artistic tradition, these institutions offer vital insights into New Mexico's complex cultural tapestry.

C. Native American Festivals and Events

New Mexico is noted for its vibrant Native American festivals and celebrations, which offer a unique opportunity to witness and appreciate the indigenous peoples' rich cultural legacy. The following are some noteworthy Native American festivals and events in New Mexico:

Gathering of Nations Powwow (Albuquerque): This is one of North America's largest powwows, bringing together Native American tribes from all over the continent. Competitive dancing, drumming, singing, traditional crafts, and food are all featured. The festival aims to promote Native American culture and foster unity among many tribes.

The Indian Market (Santa Fe) is a well-known festival that shows Native American artists' artwork, jewelry, pottery, textiles, and other traditional crafts. It is organized by the Southwestern Association for Indian Arts. It draws collectors, art enthusiasts, and tourists from all over the world.

Annual Feast Day of the Ohkay Owingeh Pueblo (Ohkay Owingeh): This traditional feast day is celebrated yearly at Ohkay Owingeh Pueblo, one of New Mexico's 19 pueblos. It is a time when the community gathers to celebrate with traditional dances, music, and feasting. Visitors are frequently invited to watch and partake in the celebrations.

The Gallup Inter-Tribal Indian Ceremonial (Gallup) is a multi-day event that includes Native American dancing competitions, arts and crafts sellers, rodeo events, and ceremonial rites. It allows visitors to learn about the cultural richness and practices of numerous Native American tribes.

Feast Day Festivals (Various Pueblos): Throughout the year, each of New Mexico's 19 Pueblos has its own unique feast days and festivals. Traditional dances, music, cuisine, and ceremonial activities are frequently included in these celebrations. San

Geronimo Feast Day at Taos Pueblo and the Corn Dance at Zuni Pueblo are two prominent feast days.

Winter Indian Market (Santa Fe): The Winter Indian Market, organized by the Southwestern Association for Indian Arts, is a smaller-scale counterpart of the Indian Market conducted throughout the winter season. It provides an opportunity to buy one-of-a-kind Native American artwork and crafts directly from the creators.

Red Earth Celebration (Albuquerque): This celebration honors the traditional legacy of Oklahoma Native American tribes, but also draws participants and visitors from all across the country, including New Mexico. Dance performances, art exhibitions, storytelling, and cultural demonstrations are all part of the festivities.

These festivals and events not only provide opportunities to see compelling performances and amazing artwork, but they also provide insights into the rich traditions and cultural practices of Native American communities. Visitors can experience the colorful spirit and ongoing traditions of New Mexico's indigenous peoples by attending these festivals.

Chapter 6: Cuisine and Culinary Delights

A. New Mexican Cuisine

New Mexican cuisine is a distinctive and tasty culinary style influenced by Native American, Spanish, Mexican, and cowboy elements. It is well-known for its robust flavors, bright spices, and utilization of locally sourced ingredients. Here are some of the essential characteristics and popular dishes of New Mexican cuisine:

Chile Peppers: Chile peppers are an essential ingredient in New Mexican cuisine. The state is well-known for its green and red chile peppers, which are used in numerous recipes. Green chile is collected sooner and has a milder flavor, but red chile is left to mature and has a richer, hotter flavor.

Enchiladas: Enchiladas are a mainstay of New Mexican cuisine. They are made up of wrapped corn tortillas filled with cheese, meat, or beans and topped with red or green chile sauce. Cheese, onions, and fried eggs are frequently added to the dish.

Tamales: Another popular New Mexican food is tamales. They are produced by placing masa (corn dough) over a corn husk, stuffing it with meat or cheese, and then steaming or baking it. Tamales are available with either red or green chile sauce.

Posole: A classic soup made with hominy (dried maize kernels treated with an alkali solution) and meat, typically pork. It is spiced and cooked until the flavors mix. Posole is frequently consumed at festive occasions and celebrations.

Carne Adovada: Carne adovada is a slow-cooked marinated pork dish. Typically, the pig is marinated in a blend of red chile, garlic, and other spices before being cooked till tender. It can be served as a main course or as a taco or burrito filling.

Sopapillas: A traditional New Mexican dessert. They are light, fluffy pastries that are fried until golden brown and puff up. Sopapillas can be eaten with honey, as a base for dishes such as sopapilla cheesecake, or as a side dish to savory meals.

Green Chile Stew: A hearty and soothing dish composed of chunks of meat (often pork), potatoes, veggies, and green chile. It's all cooked together to make a tasty and spicy stew that's ideal for cold days.

Biscochitos: Biscochitos are anise and cinnamon-flavored classic New Mexican cookies. They have a delicate texture and are popular for holidays and special events.

These are just a few of the numerous delectable meals and tastes available in New Mexican cuisine. The food reflects the region's numerous cultural influences and provides visitors and locals with a delightful culinary trip.

B. Iconic Dishes and Local Specialties

New Mexico has several renowned meals and regional delicacies that highlight the region's distinct flavors and culinary traditions. Here are some must-try New Mexican foods and specialties:

Green Chile Cheeseburger: A New Mexican Take on the Traditional Cheeseburger It has a delicious beef patty with melted cheese and roasted green chile peppers on top. The flavor combination offers a spicy and delicious treat.

Navajo Taco: The base of a Navajo taco, also known as an "Indian taco," is fry bread. The fried bread is topped with your choice of seasoned ground beef, beans, lettuce, tomatoes, cheese, and additional toppings. It's a filling and tasty supper.

Frito pie is a popular snack or dinner in New Mexico. It's made up of a bag of Fritos corn chips topped with red or green chili, cheese, onions, and other garnishes. It's a filling and savory dish that's popular at sporting events, festivals, and casual restaurants.

Sopaipillas Stuffed: Sopaipillas are fried pastries that can be eaten sweet or savory. Stuffed sopaipillas are made with ground beef, beans, cheese, and/or chile sauce. They are a popular option for a filling and tasty supper.

Carne Asada is a marinated and grilled beef dish popular in New Mexican cuisine. The beef is spice-seasoned and cooked to perfection before being served with tortillas, beans, rice, and salsa. It's a tasty and filling solution for meat lovers.

Green Chile Stew: Green Chile Stew is a traditional New Mexican dish. It usually consists of chunks of pork, potatoes, onions, and garlic cooked in a delicious broth prepared with roasted green chiles. The stew is rich and spicy, and it's ideal for keeping warm on a winter day.

Tacos al Pastor: Tacos al Pastor are popular in New Mexico and are influenced by Mexican cuisine. Thinly sliced pork is marinated in a blend of spices and pineapple before being roasted on a vertical spit. The beef is then served with onions, cilantro, and a squeeze of lime on soft tortillas.

Sopa de Albóndigas: Sopa de Albóndigas is a classic meatball soup from New Mexico. It has seasoned meatballs made from ground beef, rice, onions, and herbs that are cooked in a savory broth with vegetables such as carrots, celery, and potatoes.

These famous dishes and regional delicacies illustrate New Mexico's rich flavors and culinary traditions. Whether you favor spicy and salty foods or something sweet and indulgent, the state's diversified and exquisite cuisine has something for everyone.

C. Best Restaurants and Food Markets

New Mexico has a thriving culinary industry, with a range of outstanding restaurants and food markets where you can sample regional delicacies. Here are some of New Mexico's greatest restaurants and food markets:

Restaurants:

Restaurant Martn (Santa Fe): Restaurant Martn offers a refined dining experience with meals produced from locally obtained ingredients. It is known for its inventive and contemporary American cuisine with Southwestern elements.

The Shed (Santa Fe): The Shed is a Santa Fe institution serving authentic New Mexican food in a picturesque and historic environment. Their red and green chile sauces are well-known, and their menu includes traditional meals such as enchiladas and posole.

El Pinto (Albuquerque): El Pinto is a prominent New Mexican cuisine restaurant in Albuquerque. Their menu features a diverse selection of meals, ranging from green chile stew to stacked enchiladas, all served in a lively and joyful ambiance.

The Compound (Santa Fe): The Compound is a well-known Santa Fe gourmet dining institution. It serves a refined menu that blends classic French techniques with regional flavors, with products acquired locally whenever feasible.

Coyote Cafe (Santa Fe): Coyote Cafe is a Santa Fe culinary hotspot recognized for its inventive Southwestern cuisine. The restaurant serves a variety of dishes that combine traditional and modern ingredients, as well as an extensive wine list.

Food Market:

Santa Fe Farmers Market (Santa Fe): For foodies, the Santa Fe Farmers Market is a must-see. It sells a wide range of fresh produce, local meats, artisanal cheeses, baked goods, and other items. There are also food booths selling wonderful meals and snacks.

Los Poblanos Farm Shop (Albuquerque): Los Poblanos Farm Shop is located on an organic lavender farm and offers a curated range of locally produced products such as farm-fresh produce, artisanal cheeses, handcrafted jams, and lavender-infused products.

La Montaita Co-op (Albuquerque and Santa Fe): A community-owned grocery shop that focuses on organic and locally sourced items. They have a large selection of natural goods, including fresh vegetables, bulk items, specialized items, and a deli department.

Talin Market World Food Fare (Albuquerque): Talin Market is an international food market with a wide variety of ingredients and goods from all over the world. There is a large selection of Asian, Hispanic, and Middle Eastern cuisine, spices, and specialized items.

The Farmer's Market at the Rail Yards (Albuquerque): This lively farmers market in the historic Albuquerque Rail Yards features local farmers, food vendors, craftsmen, and live music. It's a terrific place to try out fresh vegetables, handcrafted delicacies, and one-of-a-kind items.

These restaurants and food markets offer a variety of dining experiences and opportunities to sample New Mexico's cuisine. Whether you're seeking traditional New Mexican dishes, foreign cuisine, or fresh and local ingredients to make your own culinary creations, these restaurants will satisfy your appetites while also highlighting the state's culinary diversity.

Chapter 7: Outdoor Festivals and Events

A. Albuquerque International Balloon Fiesta

The Albuquerque International Balloon Fiesta is a yearly event in Albuquerque, New Mexico. It is the world's largest hot-air balloon festival, attracting thousands of guests from all over the world. Here are some important facts regarding the balloon fiesta:

Dates and Location: The Balloon Fiesta usually takes place in early October and lasts nine days. It is hosted at Balloon Fiesta Park in Albuquerque, which is easily accessible to both locals and tourists.

Mass Ascensions: One of the Balloon Fiesta's biggest attractions is the mass ascensions, in which hundreds of colorful hot air balloons take flight at the same time. It's a stunning sight to see as the sky fills with a slew of colorful balloons, producing a breathtaking visual spectacle.

The Special Shapes Rodeo is another popular attraction at the Balloon Fiesta. This event features balloons that have been distinctively made and ingeniously shaped, ranging from animals and cartoon figures to objects and symbols. For guests of all ages, the Special Shapes Rodeo provides a creative and playful experience.

Balloon Glow: The Balloon Fiesta Park offers the Balloon Glow event in the evenings. The balloons are attached to the ground during this spectacular show while their burners are ignited, generating a dazzling glow that illuminates the night sky. Attendees have a captivating and memorable experience.

The Balloon Fiesta begins each morning with the Dawn Patrol event. Before sunrise, a small group of balloons goes off to test the wind conditions. The sight of these luminous balloons against the black sky is a lovely and peaceful scene.

Competitions and Events: The Balloon Fiesta also includes a variety of balloon pilot competitions and events. These tournaments put their navigation, precision, and speed to the test. Visitors can watch the pilots' outstanding abilities as they compete in various trials.

Family Activities: The Balloon Fiesta provides a variety of activities for families to enjoy. Carnival rides, food vendors selling a variety of local and international cuisine, live entertainment, and interactive displays are available. It has a celebratory atmosphere that appeals to people of all ages.

Photography possibilities: The Balloon Fiesta, with its brilliant balloons and picturesque settings, provides plenty of possibilities for photographers to create breathtaking shots. There are numerous picturesque moments to capture during mass ascensions, the balloon glow, or special events.

Attending the Albuquerque International Balloon Fiesta is a once-in-a-lifetime opportunity to see the majesty and grandeur of hot air balloons against the backdrop of New Mexico's terrain. It's a celebration of color, creativity, and the thrill of flying that will leave everyone who attends with unforgettable memories.

B. Santa Fe Indian Market

The Santa Fe Indian Market is an annual cultural festival conducted in Santa Fe, New Mexico. It is the world's largest and most prestigious Native American art market, organized by the

Southwestern Association for Indian Arts (SWAIA). The event draws artists, collectors, and visitors from all around the world.

Date and Location: The Santa Fe Indian Market is usually held on a weekend in August. The Santa Fe Plaza in downtown Santa Fe serves as the market's major hub.

Artwork: The market offers a diverse selection of Native American artwork, such as pottery, jewelry, textiles, paintings, sculptures, and more. The artwork reflects the rich cultural heritage of Native American tribes in both traditional and contemporary ways.

Artist stalls: Hundreds of artist stalls transform the Santa Fe Plaza into a bustling bazaar. Artists from various tribes around the United States and Canada set up stalls to sell and display their work.

Artist Interactions: Meeting the artists themselves is one of the market's attractions. Visitors can speak with the artists, learn about their processes and inspirations, and obtain a better appreciation of the cultural value of their works.

Cultural Performances: There will be cultural performances throughout the weekend that exhibit traditional Native American dances, music, and storytelling. These performances provide an enthralling peek into Native American tribes' rich cultural traditions and histories.

Food and Cuisine: The market also has food booths selling Native American cuisine. Traditional meals such as fry bread, Navajo tacos, Indian corn soup, and others are available to visitors, enabling a culinary study of Native American flavors.

Cultural interchange: The Santa Fe Indian Market promotes cultural interchange and appreciation. It allows visitors to learn about the various Native American cultures, traditions, and artistic expressions, promoting a deeper knowledge and respect for Native American heritage.

Collecting Artwork: The market provides a unique opportunity for art aficionados and collectors to obtain authentic and high-quality Native American artwork straight from the artists. This benefits the artists and ensures the survival of their traditional creative forms.

The Santa Fe Indian Market honors Native American art, culture, and ingenuity. It offers a lively and immersive experience in which visitors can interact with artists, watches exciting performances, sample Native American cuisine, and take home one-of-a-kind pieces of artwork that represent Native American tribes' rich past.

C. Gathering of Nations Powwow

The Gathering of Nations Powwow is one of the world's largest and most prominent powwows. It is a Native American cultural festival held annually in Albuquerque, New Mexico. The Gathering of Nations Powwow is summarized below:

The Gathering of Nations Dates and Location The powwow lasts three days and is usually held in late April. The event is hosted at the Tingley Coliseum on the Albuquerque Expo New Mexico fairgrounds.

The powwow's purpose and significance are to celebrate Native American culture, customs, and spirituality. It unites tribes from all around the United States, as well as Canada and other indigenous nations, together to celebrate their rich heritage via song, dance, arts and crafts, and cultural exhibitions.

The Grand Entry, a colorful and awe-inspiring procession, kicks off the powwow. Dancers dressed in vivid regalia from several tribes enter the arena to the beat of the drums, producing a dramatic and mesmerizing display. This is a time of unity and reverence, representing the gathering together of various tribes and nations.

The Gathering of Nations: Dance Competitions A variety of dance competitions are held at Powwow. Participants of all ages, from young children to seasoned dancers, demonstrate various dance styles such as traditional, fancy, jingle, and grass. The beauty, talent, and diversity of Native American dance traditions are highlighted in these competitions.

Drum Groups: Several drum groups accompany the powwow, comprising singers and drummers who provide the heartbeat and rhythm for the dancers. The drum ensembles play traditional melodies, keeping the dancers on time and generating energy and a sense of cultural pride.

Arts, goods, and exhibits: There will also be a big marketplace where Native American artisans and vendors will display and sell their goods, such as jewelry, ceramics, beadwork, textiles, and artwork. Visitors can enjoy and purchase original Native American creations, thereby supporting the artisans and their communities.

The Gathering of Nations: Cultural Education Through workshops, lectures, and interactive exhibits, Powwow promotes cultural education. Visitors can learn about traditional Native American customs, spirituality, history, and contemporary challenges affecting indigenous communities.

Food and Cuisine: Native American cuisine and traditional cuisines are available at the powwow.

Visitors can sample the scents and tastes of Native American culinary traditions, from fry bread and Indian tacos to buffalo burgers and traditional stews.

Miss Indian World Pageant: The Miss Indian World Pageant is presented as part of the powwow to honor and promote the talents, knowledge, and beauty of Native American women from various tribes. Contestants take part in a variety of cultural events, including traditional talent shows, public speaking, and interviews, all culminating in the crowning of Miss Indian World.

The Nations Gathering Powwows are dynamic and culturally enriching experiences that bring Native American tribes and people from all walks of life together. It provides a venue for the preservation and celebration of Native American traditions, as well as the promotion of cross-cultural understanding and appreciation.

D. Roswell UFO Festival

The Roswell UFO Festival is an annual event conducted in Roswell, New Mexico, commemorating the iconic 1947 Roswell UFO encounter. The following is an overview of the Roswell UFO Festival:

Dates and Location: The festival is normally held throughout a weekend in early July, near the anniversary of the Roswell UFO incident. It takes place in downtown Roswell, with a variety of activities and events taking place around the city.

The Roswell UFO incident, which involved the supposed crash of an unidentified flying object (UFO) near Roswell in 1947, is honored at the festival. The occurrence drew a lot of attention and inspired a lot of conspiracy theories and speculations over the possibility of extraterrestrial life.

Parades and Costumes: The Alien Costume Contest and the Alien Pet Contest are two of the Roswell UFO Festival's highlights. Festivalgoers dress up as aliens and parade through the streets of Roswell, exhibiting their inventiveness and appreciating the extraterrestrial theme.

Alien-themed Activities: For guests of all ages, the festival provides a variety of alien-themed activities and attractions. Live music performances, art displays, alien-themed merchants, interactive exhibits, and games are among them. Aliens-themed cuisine and drinks are also available for festivalgoers to enjoy.

Lectures & presentations: Throughout the festival, specialists, researchers, and enthusiasts will offer their knowledge and viewpoints on the Roswell incident, UFOs, and other relevant issues. These seminars allow attendees to learn about the event's history, ideas, and continuing research.

UFO Museum and Research Center: The festival takes place in conjunction with the International UFO Museum and Research Center's presence in Roswell. Visitors can tour the museum's displays, which trace the history of the Roswell incident and feature numerous items, eyewitness testimonies, and conspiracy theories.

Family Activities: The Roswell UFO Festival provides a variety of family-friendly activities and entertainment. Children's activities, face painting, bounce castles, and live music are available for younger festivalgoers.

Nighttime Events: The celebration continues after the sun goes down with spectacular nighttime events. These might include UFO-themed concerts, outdoor movies, stargazing sessions, and even light shows inspired by UFOs.

The Roswell UFO Festival draws UFO enthusiasts, conspiracy theorists, curious visitors, and families seeking a one-of-a-kind and fascinating experience. It allows guests to immerse themselves in the mystery and excitement surrounding the Roswell incident, while also enjoying the festive environment and the opportunity to meet with others who share their interests.

E. Taos Pueblo Powwow

The Taos Pueblo Powwow is an annual cultural event conducted in Taos, New Mexico, at the Taos Pueblo. It's a raucous celebration of Native American culture, dancing, music, and the arts. The following is an overview of the Taos Pueblo Powwow:

Dates and Location: The powwow is usually held on a weekend in July. The Taos Pueblo, a UNESCO World Heritage Site and one of the United States' oldest continuously inhabited villages, provides the event's backdrop.

Traditional Native American dances are performed at the powwow, including men's fancy, women's fancy shawl, traditional, grass, and jingle dances. Dancers in vibrant costumes perform precise footwork and motions to the beat of drum groups.

Drum Groups: Drum groups from several Native American tribes perform at the powwow. These bands perform traditional melodies and offer rhythmic accompaniment for the dancers, resulting in a lively and engaging ambiance.

Native American Arts & Crafts: Visitors to the event can tour a marketplace including Native American artisans and exhibitors. They display and sell a vast range of Native American tribes' cultural heritage, including jewelry, ceramics, beading, textiles, paintings, and sculptures.

Traditional Native American cuisine is a hallmark of the powwow. Delicious Native American cuisine, such as fried bread, Indian tacos, roasted corn, buffalo burgers, and other stews, is available to visitors. These delectable treats offer a distinct taste of Native American flavors and culinary traditions.

Cultural exhibitions: Cultural exhibitions during the powwow often provide insights into the history, traditions, and customs of the Taos Pueblo and other Native American tribes. Visitors can learn about the significance of traditional attire, ceremonial customs, storytelling, and indigenous language preservation.

Artistic Competitions: The powwow may include artistic competitions that allow participants to demonstrate their skills in areas like beadwork, ceramics, painting, and traditional dress. These competitions acknowledge and honor Native American artists' talents.

Community Gathering: The Taos Pueblo Powwow is a community gathering as well as a celebration of Native American culture. It allows tribal members and visitors of all backgrounds to come together, exchange stories, make relationships, and celebrate the rich heritage of Native American traditions.

Attending the Taos Pueblo Powwow provides guests with a one-of-a-kind and immersive opportunity to witness and enjoy the beauty, talent, and cultural diversity of Native American traditions. It honors the community, history, and continuing spirit of the Taos Pueblo and Native American nations.

Chapter 8: Road Trips and Scenic Drives

A. The Enchanted Circle

In northern New Mexico, the Enchanted Circle is a picturesque byway and popular road trip route. It forms a loop through scenic landscapes, lovely cities, and breathtaking mountain panoramas.

The Enchanted Circle starts in Taos, a thriving town famed for its vibrant art scene, adobe architecture, and historic Taos Pueblo. Before embarking on the drive, spend some time exploring the town's art galleries and stores, as well as sampling the local cuisine.

Taos Ski Valley: As you depart Taos, you'll pass through the stunning Sangre de Cristo Mountains and arrive at Taos Ski Valley. This world-class ski resort provides beautiful alpine scenery, superb hiking paths, and year-round outdoor activity options.

Village of Angel Fire: Continue on the circle until you reach the village of Angel Fire. Angel Fire, known for its ski resort, offers a variety of outdoor activities such as skiing, snowboarding, golfing, and hiking. Angel Fire Resort, located nearby, offers magnificent chairlift rides with panoramic views of the surrounding mountains.

Moreno Valley: Driving through Moreno Valley will provide you with breathtaking views of the mountains and rolling hills. Ranches, fishing lakes, and hiking trails dot this gorgeous valley. It's a nice spot for a picnic or a little trek to take in the natural beauty of the area.

Red River: The beautiful town of Red River is the next stop on the Enchanted Circle. Red River, located in a valley surrounded by mountains, offers a variety of outdoor activities such as hiking, fishing, horseback riding, and off-road experiences. The town itself offers a charming, rustic ambiance, complete with stores, restaurants, and lodging.

Questa and the Rio Grande del Norte National Monument: As you continue on the loop, you'll travel through Questa and have the opportunity to explore the Rio Grande del Norte National Monument. This protected area provides spectacular views of the Rio Grande Gorge, hiking trails, and possibilities for wildlife viewing.

Return to Taos: After completing the loop, you'll return to Taos, where you can explore more of the town's attractions, visit art museums, sample the local cuisine, or simply unwind in the laid-back ambiance.

The Enchanted Circle has a wide variety of landscapes, outdoor activities, and cultural events to offer. This road trip is sure to engage and inspire you, whether you're looking for outdoor experiences, scenic beauty, or a glimpse into the region's rich legacy. Bring your camera to capture the breathtaking mountain views and wonderful atmosphere of the Enchanted Circle.

B. Turquoise Trail

The Turquoise Trail is a picturesque byway in New Mexico that connects Albuquerque and Santa Fe. It takes you on an enthralling tour across the heart of the state, through stunning landscapes, old mining towns, and different cultural sites. Here's what to expect if you travel the Turquoise Trail:

Begin in Albuquerque: Begin your tour in Albuquerque, New Mexico's largest city. Visit the city's vibrant downtown district, the historic Old Town, and experience the city's unique blend of Native American, Hispanic, and Western traditions.

As you depart Albuquerque, you'll be entering the stunning scenery of the Sandia Mountains. The route passes through picturesque gorges and woodlands, providing breathtaking views of the harsh terrain. Along the walk, keep a lookout for wildlife such as deer and birds.

Tijeras and Cedar Crest: Tijeras and Cedar Crest are the first towns you'll come across on the Turquoise Trail. These settlements give an insight into New Mexico's mining past as well as outdoor activities such as hiking and horseback riding in the surrounding forests.

Madrid: The next stop is Madrid, a unique and creative city. Madrid, once a coal mining town, has evolved into a creative community packed with art galleries, one-of-a-kind stores, and attractive cafes. Enjoy the bohemian atmosphere by strolling around the town's colorful streets.

Cerrillos: Continue on the trail until you reach the medieval village of Cerrillos. This former mining town is famed for its abundant turquoise deposits, and you may visit local stores that sell turquoise jewelry and other Southwest products. Hiking pathways and panoramic views of the surrounding landscapes may be found in Cerrillos Hills State Park.

Santa Fe: The Turquoise Trail concludes in Santa Fe, the capital of New Mexico and a city known for its art, culture, and architecture. Immerse yourself in the bustling art scene, world-class museums, the historic Plaza, and the numerous culinary offerings.

Side journeys: The Turquoise Trail provides possibilities for side journeys to natural wonders such as the Sandia Peak Tramway, which provides panoramic views of the region, and the Pecos National Historical Park, where you may learn about the area's Native American and Spanish colonial history.

The Turquoise Trail is a picturesque and cultural tour through New Mexico's landscapes, mining history, and artistic communities that have blossomed along the path. The Turquoise Trail is a must-see location for travelers looking for an authentic New Mexico experience, thanks to its diverse attractions and gorgeous environment.

C. High Road to Taos

The High Road to Taos is a picturesque route from Santa Fe to Taos, a historic town in northern New Mexico. This lovely road passes through picturesque scenery and charming Spanish settlements, providing glimpses of Native American and Spanish colonial heritage. Here's what to expect if you take the High Road to Taos:

Begin your tour in Santa Fe, a city known for its vibrant culture, rich art scene, and adobe architecture. Spend some time exploring the city's historic Plaza, visiting art galleries, and being immersed in the city's distinctive blend of Native American and Spanish influences.

Nambe and Pojoaque Pueblos: The road out of Santa Fe passes past the Native American pueblos of Nambe and Pojoaque. These villages have retained their cultural legacy, and you can tour historic adobe structures, see traditional dances, and shop at local artisan stores.

Chimayo: The village of Chimayo is one of the High Road's attractions. El Santuario de Chimayo, a prominent pilgrimage site and place of spiritual significance, is known for its medieval church. Explore the church and its surroundings, and make sure to eat the famed red chile at one of the local restaurants.

Truchas and Las Trampas: As you go further along the path, you'll come across the charming settlements of Truchas and Las Trampas. With beautiful adobe homes, antique churches, and traditional farming practices, these Spanish towns provide insights into the region's colonial past. Take a walk through the villages to experience the area's pastoral beauty.

Taos: The High Road ends in Taos, which is known for its art colony, historic adobe architecture, and the UNESCO World Heritage Site, Taos Pueblo. Explore the town's galleries, pay a visit to the Kit Carson Home and Museum, and become immersed in the bustling art scene. Don't pass up the chance to explore Taos Pueblo, an ancient Native American settlement that has been inhabited for over a thousand years.

Side Trips: Along the High Road, you can take excursions to see sights like the Rio Grande Gorge Bridge, which provides stunning views of the dramatic gorge, and the Carson National Forest, which has hiking trails and beautiful magnificence.

The High Road to Taos provides an enthralling tour through the landscapes and cultural history of New Mexico. This magnificent trip allows you to explore the region's beauty and diversity, from the creative heart of Santa Fe to the ancient traditions of Taos Pueblo. Take your time to enjoy the lovely communities, historic sites, and distinct ambiance of the High Road to Taos.

D. El Camino Real Heritage Center

The El Camino Real Heritage Center, located in Socorro, New Mexico, is a cultural and historical site. It honors the rich history and heritage of El Camino Real de Tierra Adentro, a major commercial route and road that connected Mexico City and Santa Fe during the Spanish colonial period. When you visit the El Camino Real Heritage Center, you can expect to see the following:

Exhibits and informative Displays: The historical center houses several exhibits and informative displays that provide information about El Camino Real's history and significance. Learn about the route's significance as a trade and communication corridor, its impact on the movement of products and ideas, and its role in molding New Mexico's cultural landscape.

Historic relics: The center houses a collection of El Camino Real-related historic relics. Tools, swords, pottery, and other items provide a look into the daily lives of the people who traveled and lived along the road.

Cultural and educational events are available at the El Camino Real Legacy Center to encourage awareness and appreciation of the region's history and legacy. Workshops, lectures, demonstrations, and performances highlighting the different cultures and customs along the El Camino Real may be part of these activities.

The history center offers an outdoor interpretive walk where visitors can explore the natural surroundings and learn more about the region's flora, animals, and geology. There should be instructive signage and markers along the trail that provide further historical and ecological information.

Visitors can get information about El Camino Real and other neighboring attractions at the visitor center. Staff or volunteers who are knowledgeable about the area can answer inquiries, provide maps and brochures, and provide directions for further exploration.

Gift store: The gift store of the El Camino Real Heritage Center sells books, artwork, crafts, and souvenirs relating to the trail and the region's history. It's a terrific spot to find one-of-a-kind souvenirs to remember your visit.

The El Camino Real Heritage Center provides an opportunity to learn about the interesting history and cultural significance of El Camino Real de Tierra Adentro. It's an opportunity to learn more about the region's history, connect with its rich heritage, and appreciate the significance of this ancient trading route in the formation of New Mexico.

Chapter 9: Shopping and Art Galleries

A Santa Fe Plaza

Santa Fe Plaza is the ancient heart and spirit of Santa Fe, New Mexico. It is a bustling meeting spot steeped in history, culture, and charm. Here's what to expect when you visit Santa Fe Plaza:

Historic Landmark: Santa Fe Plaza is a National Historic Landmark that dates back to the city's establishment in 1610. For generations, it has served as a central gathering area for inhabitants and visitors, as well as a hub of trade, government, and cultural activities.

The Plaza is flanked by exquisite Spanish colonial-style structures, notably the historic Palace of the Governors. The oldest continually occupied public building in the United States, this ancient adobe structure houses exhibitions on New Mexico's history and Native American art.

Shopping and Galleries: The Plaza is a shopper's dream, with various shops, boutiques, and galleries. Explore the diverse choices, which include Native American crafts and jewelry, as well as local artwork, ceramics, and one-of-a-kind Southwestern gifts. You'll discover everything from traditional crafts to contemporary art, representing Santa Fe's thriving artistic community.

Dining and Restaurants: Santa Fe Plaza has a wide range of dining alternatives to suit every taste. You can indulge in a wide range of flavors and gastronomic delights, from fancy restaurants serving New Mexican cuisine to quaint cafes and eateries. Don't pass up the opportunity to try typical New Mexican cuisine such as green chile stew or flavorful enchiladas.

Festivals & Events: Throughout the year, Santa Fe Plaza serves as a venue for a variety of festivals, markets, and events. There's always something going on in the Plaza, from the Santa Fe Indian Market, which showcases Native American art and culture, to the Santa Fe Bandstand summer concert series. Check the local events calendar to see whether there will be a festival or celebration during your visit.

Cultural Attractions: The Plaza is surrounded by cultural attractions in addition to the Palace of the Governors. Explore the Cathedral Basilica of St. Francis of Assisi, a spectacular example of Spanish colonial architecture, or the New Mexico Museum of Art, which holds a remarkable collection of Southwestern art.

Relaxation and People-Watching: Santa Fe Plaza is a great spot to unwind, soak in the ambiance and people-watch. The Plaza is littered with benches and shaded spaces that are ideal for relaxing, reading a book, or simply taking in the sights and sounds of this vibrant gathering place.

Santa Fe Plaza is the city's heart, combining history, culture, shopping, dining, and entertainment. Santa Fe Plaza is a must-see site that embodies the spirit of Santa Fe's unique charm and character, whether you're perusing the stores, immersing yourself in the local art scene, or simply enjoying the ambiance.

B. Native American Jewelry and Crafts

The beauty, artistry, and cultural significance of Native American jewelry and crafts are well known. Indigenous tribes in New Mexico and around the United States have long made elaborate jewelry, pottery, textiles, and other crafts that represent their cultural traditions and artistic abilities. Here's a look at some Native American jewelry and crafts:

Native American jewelry is in high demand due to its superb craftsmanship and use of natural materials. To make attractive items, sterling silver is frequently paired with gemstones like as turquoise, coral, onyx, and opal. Intricate silverwork, overlay techniques, stamping, and inlay work are common features of traditional designs. Each tribe has its own style, with Navajo, Zuni, and Hopi jewelry being especially well-known. Necklaces, bracelets, earrings, rings, and belt buckles are examples of common jewelry pieces.

Native American pottery is noted for its distinctive designs and techniques. Each tribe has its own ceramic style, with the Acoma, Santa Clara, and Jemez Pueblos of New Mexico being particularly well-known for their pottery traditions. Hand-coiled earthenware is generally painted with natural colors and minerals. Traditional themes frequently depict tribally significant symbols and legends. Pottery can include both aesthetic and useful items such as bowls, jars, and figures.

Textiles: Native American textiles highlight the diverse tribes' varied weaving traditions. Rugs and blankets made by Navajo weavers are prized for their unique patterns and brilliant colors. They are frequently manufactured using traditional methods, such as a vertical loom, and natural fibers such as wool. Other tribes, such as the Pueblo and Apache, have weaving traditions of their own, making magnificent textiles for clothing, blankets, and ceremonial objects.

Basketry is another major Native American craft that demonstrates the cultures' talents and creativity. Baskets have traditionally been manufactured from natural materials such as willow, yucca, and pine needles. Weaving techniques differ throughout tribes, resulting in a diverse spectrum of basket patterns and motifs.

Baskets can be used for both practical and ceremonial purposes, and they are frequently decorated with elaborate designs and motifs.

Beadwork: Many Native American tribes perform beadwork as a traditional craft. Intricate designs are created by hand-sewing colorful glass or metal beads onto leather or fabric. Beadwork can be found on garments, moccasins, bags, and jewelry, among other things. Each tribe has its own style of beadwork, with motifs that frequently include tribal emblems, animals, or geometric patterns.

It is critical to support authentic Native American craftsmen and buy from reliable suppliers when purchasing Native American jewelry and crafts. Look for authenticity certifications and buy directly from tribal-owned businesses, galleries, or cooperatives. These purchases not only benefit the craftsmen and their communities, but they also assure that you are purchasing authentic and responsibly obtained Native American art.

Native American jewelry and crafts offer an insight into indigenous communities' rich cultural heritage and aesthetic traditions. Owning or wearing these works helps you to connect with the stories, symbolism, and craftsmanship that have been passed down through the centuries, making them treasured and meaningful works of art.

C. Art Markets and Galleries

New Mexico is known for its thriving art scene, and there are various art fairs and galleries throughout the state where you can explore and buy a variety of artistic products. Here are some noteworthy art markets and galleries to check out:

Santa Fe Indian Market: The Santa Fe Indian Market, held annually in Santa Fe, is one of the world's largest and most prominent Native American art markets. It exhibits the work of Native American artisans from many tribes, with a wide range of traditional and contemporary art, jewelry, ceramics, textiles, and other items.

The Spanish Market, which is also held in Santa Fe, honors New Mexico's rich Hispanic heritage. Woodcarving, tinwork, weaving, ironwork, and furniture are examples of traditional Spanish Colonial art. The market offers a one-of-a-kind opportunity to admire the skills and traditions of New Mexico's Spanish colonial artists.

The International Folk Art Market, held in Santa Fe, brings together artists from all over the world to present their traditional crafts and artwork. This market provides an intriguing peek into many countries' diverse cultures and artistic traditions, including textiles, ceramics, jewelry, and other folk art.

Canyon Road in Santa Fe is well-known for its concentration of art establishments. Stroll down this scenic street lined with adobe structures to see a variety of galleries displaying works by local, national, and international artists. Canyon Road has a broad range of artistic expressions, ranging from contemporary to traditional Southwestern works.

Railyard Arts District, Santa Fe: The Railyard Arts District in Santa Fe is another popular destination for art lovers. This redeveloped neighborhood is home to contemporary art galleries, studios, and exhibition spaces. Explore the vibrant art scene, attend art openings and events, and meet emerging artists pushing the envelope in a variety of genres.

Taos Art Colony: Taos has long been a sanctuary for artists, attracting luminaries such as Georgia O'Keeffe and R.C. Gorman. Numerous galleries in town display a diverse spectrum of artwork, including paintings, sculptures, pottery, and photography. Explore the Taos Art Colony to become immersed in the thriving artistic community and appreciate the town's distinct creative energy.

Albuquerque's Old Town is a lovely historic quarter filled with adobe structures, boutiques, and galleries. Local artists display their work here, including paintings, ceramics, jewelry, and other items. Browse the art galleries while learning about the city's rich history and culture.

Gallup Art Market: The Gallup Art Market, located in Gallup, New Mexico, is a bustling market displaying Native American art and crafts. Jewelry, ceramics, weavings, and other traditional and contemporary Native American artwork are available. The market allows visitors to interact with

Native American artists and learn about their creative processes.

Exploring New Mexico's art markets and galleries allows you to immerse yourself in the state's lively artistic community and find unique and fascinating masterpieces. These galleries provide a diverse range of artistic expressions to admire and collect, whether you're seeking traditional Native American art, modern items, or international folk art.

D. Unique Souvenirs and Local Products

When visiting New Mexico, there are various unique souvenirs and local products to consider purchasing as souvenirs. These things highlight the state's diverse culture, heritage, and cuisine. Here are some examples:

Native American pottery from New Mexico's numerous tribes, such as the Acoma, Santa Clara, and Jemez Pueblos, is a popular choice. Look for handcrafted pottery with elaborate designs and bright colors. Each tribe has its own style and skills, making these clay pieces one-of-a-kind and special.

Native American jewelry is highly sought after and makes an excellent keepsake. Look for works by Navajo, Zuni, or Hopi artists. Sterling silver is frequently used in conjunction with gemstones such as turquoise, coral, and onyx. Choose from necklaces, bracelets, earrings, or rings, each highlighting Native American jewelry's artistry and cultural significance.

Chile & Spices: New Mexico is known for its chile peppers, and you can bring home a variety of chile-based items. Look for chile sauce, chile powder, or chile-infused seasonings in jars. With these flavorful ingredients, you can recreate the distinct flavor of New Mexican food in your own kitchen.

Native American Crafts: Other than pottery and jewelry, Native American crafts are worth investigating. Handwoven carpets, baskets, and textiles reflect tribal weaving traditions such as the Navajo, Pueblo, and Apache. Popular items include beadwork, dreamcatchers, and kachina dolls.

Traditional Blankets and Carpets: The Navajo people are well-known for their traditional blankets and carpets. Intricate designs and brilliant hues adorn these handwoven rugs. To add a bit of Southwest character to your house, look for real Navajo rugs or blankets.

Chimayo Blankets and Shawls: Chimayo is a small community in New Mexico that is well-known for its handmade textiles. Chimayo blankets and shawls are well-known for their high quality and distinctive designs. Consider investing in one of these wonderful outfits to keep you warm and fashionable throughout the winter months.

Traditional Native American Flute or Drum: If you enjoy music, try getting a traditional Native American flute or drum. These instruments have a deep cultural history and might be a one-of-a-kind addition to your musical collection.

Local Artwork: Because New Mexico has a vibrant art scene, consider purchasing local artwork as a keepsake. There is a vast spectrum of artistic forms that represent the spirit of the state, whether it is a painting, sculpture, or photography.

Handcrafted Pottery and Ceramics: Look for locally manufactured handcrafted pottery and ceramics. These one-of-a-kind objects might range from ornamental vases and bowls to useful mugs and plates. Each piece bears the artist's creative touch and brings a touch of New Mexican artistry to your house.

Specialty Foods and Drinks: New Mexico is recognized for its gastronomic delights, so carry some home with you. Look for New Mexican salsa, honey, and bottles of local wine or craft beer. These delectable delights allow you to appreciate the flavors of New Mexico long after your visit.

Consider visiting local markets, Native American-owned shops, or galleries that support local craftspeople when looking for souvenirs and local products. These locations allow visitors to interact with the artisans and learn about the cultural significance of the products. By purchasing one-of-a-kind souvenirs and local products, you not only bring home significant memories but also help to support the local economy and maintain New Mexico's heritage and traditions.

Chapter 10: Family-Friendly Attractions

A. Albuquerque BioPark

The Albuquerque Biological Park is a popular family attraction that offers a wide range of exciting experiences. More information about the park's many attractions may be found here:

The Albuquerque Zoo is home to a diverse collection of species from throughout the world. Families may see elephants, giraffes, lions, tigers, bears, and other creatures in exhibits. There are also educational presentations, animal interactions, and a Children's Farm at the zoo where children can interact with domestic animals.

ABQ BioPark Aquarium: In the aquarium, visitors can learn about the wonders of marine life. Discover exhibits that showcase distinct aquatic ecosystems, such as the Amazon jungle, coral reefs, and the Gulf of Mexico. Families may marvel at the colorful fish, sharks, jellyfish, and seahorses, and even touch stingrays in the interactive touch pool.

ABQ BioPark Botanic Garden: The botanic garden offers a tranquil and beautiful place for families to enjoy. Explore the Japanese Garden, the Mediterranean Conservatory, and the Children's Fantasy Garden, among others. Children will enjoy the Children's Fantasy Garden, which features colorful sculptures, a butterfly garden, and interactive exhibits.

Tingley Beach is a recreational area with ponds near the zoo where families may enjoy fishing, picnics, and hiking along the beautiful trails. There is also a model boating pond where guests can sail their own model boats.

Throughout the year, the Albuquerque Biological Park also hosts unique events and educational programs for families. Summer camps, wildlife protection programs, and seasonal events, such as the River of Lights during the holiday season, are among them.

The Albuquerque Biological Park is both enjoyable and educational for the whole family. With animals, aquatic life, botanical gardens, and outdoor sports, this place has something for everyone.

B. New Mexico Museum of Natural History and Science

The New Mexico Museum of Natural History and Science is a fascinating Albuquerque attraction. Here's a rundown of what visitors to this family-friendly museum can expect:

Exhibits: The museum houses a diverse collection of exhibits that highlight the natural history and scientific wonders of New Mexico and the world at large. Exhibits on dinosaurs, fossils, minerals, geology, paleontology, anthropology, and space exploration are available to visitors. The interactive and engaging exhibits allow visitors to learn through hands-on experiences.

DynaTheater: The museum houses the DynaTheater, a cutting-edge giant-screen theater that features immersive and educational films. Visitors can watch stunning documentaries on topics such as nature, science, and space exploration. The large screen and powerful sound system in the theater provide an enthralling cinematic experience.

Planetarium: The Planetarium at the museum takes visitors on a journey through the cosmos. Immersive planetariums shows explore the wonders of the universe, such as stars, galaxies, planets, and the solar system. The shows are informative and help viewers gain a better understanding of space and astronomy.

Hands-on Learning and Interactive Experiences: The museum promotes hands-on learning and interactive experiences. Throughout the museum, visitors can participate in a variety of activities and demonstrations, such as fossil digging, interactive displays, and educational games. For visitors of all ages, these interactive elements make the learning experience more engaging and enjoyable.

Education Programs: For children, families, and school groups, the museum offers educational programs and workshops. These programs offer opportunities for more in-depth exploration and learning in a structured and guided setting. These programs, which range from science experiments to educational presentations, enhance the overall museum experience.

Gift Shop: The museum's gift shop sells educational toys, books, fossils, minerals, and science-themed merchandise. It's a fantastic place to find one-of-a-kind souvenirs and gifts related to the museum's exhibits and themes. Visitors who want to take a piece of the museum home with them frequent the gift shop.

Families will find the New Mexico Museum of Natural History and Science to be both educational and entertaining. It combines education, exploration, and hands-on activities to foster a greater understanding and appreciation of nature and scientific discoveries. This museum has something for everyone, whether you're interested in dinosaurs, space exploration, or New Mexico geology.

C. Meow Wolf

Meow Wolf is a one-of-a-kind and immersive art experience in Santa Fe, New Mexico. What you need to know about this one-of-a-kind attraction is as follows:

The House of Eternal Return: The main installation of Meow Wolf is called "The House of Eternal Return." It's a massive interactive art installation that takes visitors on a surreal and mind-bending journey. The exhibit is housed in what appears to be an ordinary Victorian house, but once inside, you'll find yourself in a fantastical and mysterious world.

Meow Wolf's installations are well-known for their interactive elements. Touching, climbing, and exploring the various rooms and spaces is encouraged. Throughout the exhibition, you can open drawers, crawl through secret passages, and discover hidden surprises. It's a place where art comes to life, and you become a part of the experience.

Multidimensional Narrative: The immersive environments of The House of Eternal Return tell a captivating story. Each room and space is meticulously designed, with intricate details and clues that add to the overall narrative. You'll discover pieces of the story as you explore, and you'll be able to piece together the mystery behind the house's bizarre and otherworldly elements.

Collaborations in the Arts: Meow Wolf is known for its collaborative approach to art. The exhibition showcases the work of a group of artists, musicians, designers, and storytellers. It's a synthesis of various creative disciplines that results in a visually stunning and immersive experience. As you walk through the exhibit, you'll come across a wide range of art styles and mediums.

Events and Performances: Throughout the year, Meow Wolf hosts a variety of events and performances. Live music, DJ sets, theatrical performances, workshops, and other activities are available. The events enhance the Meow Wolf experience by adding an extra layer of excitement and entertainment, allowing visitors to interact with the art in new and dynamic ways.

Gift Shop and Café: Check out Meow Wolf's gift shop before or after your visit for unique merchandise, art prints, and quirky souvenirs. There is also a café on-site where you can get a bite to eat or a drink.

Meow Wolf provides a truly immersive and awe-inspiring art experience for people of all ages. It's a place where imagination and wonder reign supreme, and visitors are invited to immerse themselves in it. Meow Wolf is a must-see destination in Santa Fe, New Mexico, whether you're an art enthusiast, a curious explorer, or simply looking for a memorable and unusual experience.

D. Rio Grande Nature Center State Park

Rio Grande Nature Center State Park is a lovely and peaceful natural area in Albuquerque, New Mexico. Here's what you can expect if you go to this nature park:

Nature Trails: Several nature trails wind through the park's diverse ecosystems along the Rio Grande River. These trails allow visitors to immerse themselves in nature and observe the local flora and fauna. You can take leisurely walks along the trails, admire the scenery, and even spot various bird species that live in the area.

Birdwatching: Rio Grande Nature Center State Park is a birdwatcher's paradise. The park attracts a wide variety of birds throughout the year due to its prime location along the migratory path of many bird species. Birdwatchers can see sandhill cranes, great blue herons, bald eagles, and many other species. To enhance the birdwatching experience, the park provides viewing platforms and educational programs.

The park has a visitor center with informative exhibits and displays about the natural history and wildlife of the Rio Grande Valley. Inside the visitor center, you can learn about the area's unique ecosystems, the significance of river conservation, and the various species that live there. The knowledgeable staff is also on hand to answer any questions and offer suggestions for exploring the park.

Rio Grande Nature Center State Park provides educational programs and workshops for visitors of all ages. Environmental conservation, wildlife education, and hands-on learning experiences are the focus of these programs. Guided walks, nature talks, and interactive activities promote a deeper understanding and appreciation of the natural world for families and school groups.

Wildlife Viewing: In addition to birdwatching, the park is home to a variety of other wildlife species. Visitors might see rabbits, coyotes, lizards, and a variety of amphibians and reptiles. The natural habitats of the park offer numerous opportunities for wildlife observation and photography.

Picnic Areas: Rio Grande Nature Center State Park has designated picnic areas where visitors can relax, eat, and enjoy the tranquil surroundings. These areas, which include tables, benches, and shade, are ideal for a family picnic or a quiet break during your visit.

Rio Grande Nature Center State Park offers a serene escape within the city of Albuquerque, whether you're a nature lover, a bird enthusiast, or simply looking for a peaceful retreat. It's a place to reconnect with nature, learn about local ecosystems, and appreciate the Rio Grande Valley's natural beauty.

E. Explora Science Center and Children's Museum

Explora Science Center and Children's Museum, located in Albuquerque, New Mexico, is dynamic and interactive. What to expect when visiting this interesting educational institution:

Hands-on Exhibits: Explora has a variety of hands-on exhibits designed to pique children's and adults' interests and inspire learning. These exhibits cover a wide range of scientific disciplines, such as physics, biology, chemistry, engineering, and others.

Visitors can participate in interactive activities, experiments, and simulations designed to make learning enjoyable and memorable.

Activities in Science and Technology: The museum provides a variety of science and technology activities that encourage experimentation and exploration. Workshops, science demonstrations, and make-and-take projects are available to visitors. These activities allow students to delve deeper into scientific concepts while also developing problem-solving skills.

Explora has an outdoor Science Park where visitors can see scientific principles in action. The park has interactive exhibits that explore topics like motion, energy, and natural forces. Visitors can engage in water play, structure construction, and outdoor physics experiments.

Early Childhood Programs: Explora caters to younger children with special programs and exhibits. Sensory exploration, motor skill development, and imaginative play are the focus of these areas. The museum provides a safe haven for young children to explore the wonders of science and satisfy their curiosity.

The museum's Maker Space provides visitors with a creative and collaborative environment in which to engage in hands-on making and tinkering. Visitors can create and innovate using a variety of tools, materials, and technology. It's a place where creativity and imagination can flourish.

Explora's Science Theater features entertaining and educational live shows and demonstrations. Interactive science performances, demonstrations, and even science-themed storytelling are available to visitors. The theater creates a lively and immersive environment in which scientific concepts come to life.

Explora provides a variety of amenities to enhance the visitor experience. There is a café where you can get a snack or meal, a gift shop with science-themed toys and books, and relaxing and reflective areas.

Explora Science Center and Children's Museum offer a dynamic and engaging environment in which children and adults can explore and discover the wonders of science. It's a place where learning is transformed into an interactive adventure and where curiosity is fostered. Explora offers a stimulating and educational journey for visitors of all ages, whether they are interested in physics, biology, or chemistry, or simply enjoy hands-on learning experiences.

Chapter 11: Outdoor Recreation and Adventure Sports

A. Skiing and Snowboarding

Because of the state's beautiful mountain ranges and plentiful snowfall, skiing and snowboarding are popular winter activities in New Mexico. What you need to know about skiing and snowboarding in the area is as follows:

Ski Resorts: Several ski resorts in New Mexico provide excellent terrain for both skiing and snowboarding. Taos Ski Valley, in the Sangre de Cristo Mountains, is famous for its difficult slopes and steep chutes. Ski Santa Fe, located just outside of Santa Fe, has a variety of trails suitable for skiers of all abilities. Angel Fire Resort, located in Moreno Valley, offers a family-friendly atmosphere with a variety of slopes for all skill levels.

Terrain and Trails: The terrain at New Mexico's ski resorts includes groomed runs, moguls, glades, and terrain parks. You'll find trails to suit your skill level, whether you're a beginner, intermediate, or advanced skier or snowboarder. There's something for everyone, from gentle slopes for learning and progression to challenging black diamond runs for experienced riders.

Snow Conditions: The ski season in New Mexico typically runs from November to April, depending on snowfall. The resorts supplement natural snowfall with snowmaking equipment, ensuring consistent coverage throughout the season. While the state may not receive as much snow as some other popular ski destinations, the resorts work hard to keep skiing and snowboarding conditions as good as possible.

Ski and snowboard lessons are available for all ages and abilities if you are new to skiing or snowboarding or want to improve your skills. Certified instructors can walk you through the fundamentals or help you fine-tune your technique. Private and group lessons are available, allowing you to tailor your learning experience to your specific requirements.

Rental and Services: If you do not own ski or snowboard equipment, you can rent it from the resorts or nearby rental shops. They offer a variety of equipment, such as skis, snowboards, boots, and helmets. Additionally, the resorts have shops where you can buy or rent additional accessories such as goggles, gloves, and outerwear.

On-Mountain Amenities: New Mexico ski resorts provide a variety of amenities to enhance your experience. There are cafeterias, restaurants, and snack bars where you can refuel and relax. Some resorts offer ski-in/ski-out accommodations, making it easy to get to the slopes. There are also ski schools, equipment repair shops, and rental facilities on-site.

Après-Ski and Off-Mountain Activities: New Mexico's ski resorts provide a variety of après-ski activities after a day on the slopes. Relax in a cozy lodge, listen to live music, or soak in a hot tub to unwind. If you're looking for activities away from the mountain, nearby towns and cities frequently have restaurants, shops, art galleries, and cultural attractions to explore.

Whether you're a seasoned skier or snowboarder or just starting, New Mexico's ski resorts offer winter fun and adventure. Skiing and snowboarding in New Mexico provide a memorable winter experience with stunning mountain scenery and a variety of slopes to suit all abilities.

B. River Rafting and Kayaking

River rafting and kayaking in New Mexico provide thrilling adventures amid stunning natural scenery. Here's what you need to know about the state's water activities:

Rivers and Waterways: There are several rivers and waterways in New Mexico that are ideal for rafting and kayaking. The Rio Grande and Rio Chama rivers are the two main rivers where you can participate in these activities. These rivers wind through scenic canyons, providing exciting rapids and calm stretches for paddlers of all skill levels.

Rafting and Kayaking Trips: A variety of outfitters offer guided rafting and kayaking trips on New Mexico's rivers. You can find trips suited to your skill level whether you're a beginner or an experienced paddler. Equipment rental, safety briefings, and experienced guides who provide instruction and ensure a safe and enjoyable experience are common features of guided trips.

Rapids and Difficulty Levels: The rivers in New Mexico have a variety of rapids with varying degrees of difficulty. The rapids are graded according to the International Scale of River Difficulty, with Class I being the easiest and Class V being the most difficult. Beginners can choose calmer sections with Class I or II rapids, while experienced paddlers can take on Class III or IV rapids.

Scenic Floats: If you prefer a more relaxed and scenic experience, you can go on river float trips. These trips take you through calm sections of the river, where you can take in the natural beauty, wildlife, and serenity of the surrounding landscapes. It's a great way to get out in nature and enjoy the sights and sounds of the river.

Multi-Day Expeditions: For a more immersive adventure, multi-day rafting or kayaking expeditions on rivers such as the Rio Chama are available. These trips provide the opportunity to explore remote sections of the river, camp under the stars, and spend time in the wilderness. It's an excellent way to disconnect from the modern world and immerse yourself in nature's tranquillity.

Safety and Equipment: When going rafting or kayaking, safety should always come first. Choose a reputable outfitter who prioritizes safety, provides appropriate safety equipment, and hires experienced guides. It is critical to follow the safety instructions and guidelines provided by the guides and to wear appropriate equipment, such as life jackets and helmets.

Season and Water Levels: The best time for river rafting and kayaking in New Mexico is typically in the spring and early summer when snowmelt and mountain runoff result in higher water levels. The precise timing will depend on weather conditions and dam water releases. It is best to consult with local outfitters to determine the best time for your desired river trip.

River rafting and kayaking in New Mexico provide thrilling experiences amid breathtaking natural beauty. Whether you're looking for adrenaline-pumping rapids or a peaceful float down the river, the state's rivers offer unforgettable water adventures.

C. Hot Air Ballooning

Hot air ballooning in New Mexico is a one-of-a-kind and breathtaking way to see the state's scenic beauty and vast landscapes. What you need to know about hot air ballooning in New Mexico is as follows:

Albuquerque International Balloon Fiesta: The Albuquerque International Balloon Fiesta is one of the world's most well-known hot-air balloon events. It is held every October and attracts hundreds of colorful balloons as well as thousands of visitors from all over the world. The fiesta includes mass ascensions, night glows, and various competitions, resulting in a magical sky spectacle.

While the Balloon Fiesta is a highlight, hot air ballooning is available in New Mexico year-round. The state's pleasant weather, clear skies, and diverse landscapes make it an ideal destination for balloonists. Throughout the year, various companies offer balloon rides, allowing you to soar above the scenic vistas at any time.

Launch Locations: Depending on the company and weather conditions, ballooning adventures in New Mexico can take off from a variety of locations. Launch sites in Albuquerque, Santa Fe, Taos, and other areas provide breathtaking views of the surrounding landscapes. Each location has its own distinct personality, and you can choose the one that best suits your preferences and itinerary.

Hot air balloon rides are a relaxing and peaceful way to see the beauty of New Mexico from above. As you soar into the sky, you'll be treated to breathtaking views of mountains, deserts, canyons, and sprawling landscapes. The gentle movement of the balloon allows for a peaceful journey with plenty of opportunities for photography and admiring the scenery.

Sunrise and Sunset Flights: Balloon rides are frequently scheduled during sunrise or sunset because these times of day provide the best weather and lighting for photography. Floating through the sky as the sun paints the horizon with vibrant colors is an unforgettable experience.

Safety and Experienced Pilots: Safety is of the utmost importance in hot air ballooning. Companies in New Mexico employ licensed and certified pilots with extensive experience. They follow strict safety protocols, conduct pre-flight safety briefings, and make sure all necessary equipment is in good working order. You can rest assured that your flight will be conducted following the highest safety standards.

Balloon rides in New Mexico typically last about an hour, though the entire experience, including preparation and landing, may take several hours. Prices vary depending on the company, location, and package selected. It's best to reserve your balloon ride ahead of time, especially during peak seasons or special events.

Hot air ballooning in New Mexico is a peaceful and awe-inspiring experience that allows you to appreciate the state's natural beauty from a new perspective. Whether you choose to take part in the Albuquerque International Balloon Fiesta or go on a year-round balloon ride, you'll make unforgettable memories floating above New Mexico's breathtaking landscapes.

D. Horseback Riding and Biking

Horseback riding and biking are fantastic ways to explore New Mexico's scenic beauty and diverse landscapes. Here's what you need to know about horseback riding and biking adventures in the state:

Horseback Riding:

Ranches and Stables: There are numerous ranches and stables in New Mexico that offer horseback riding experiences. These facilities offer well-trained horses, experienced guides, and a variety of trail options for riders of all skill levels.

Trail Options: Whether you're a beginner or an experienced rider, there are trails to suit your skill level and preferences. New Mexico's trails provide a variety of experiences, ranging from gentle rides through meadows and valleys to more difficult routes through rugged terrain.

Horseback riding allows you to immerse yourself in the natural beauty of New Mexico. Ride through rolling hills, high desert landscapes, pine forests, or along riverbanks. You'll have the chance to take in the breathtaking scenery, spot wildlife, and relax in the quiet of nature.

Guided Tours: Choosing a guided horseback riding tour is a great way to ensure a safe and enjoyable experience. Knowledgeable guides will lead you along the trails, provide information about the surroundings, and ensure that you have the necessary skills to handle the horses.

Horseback riding tours can last anywhere from a few hours to a full day. Prices vary depending on the length of the ride, the location, and any additional services included, such as meals or transportation. It is best to book your horseback riding excursion in advance, especially during peak seasons.

Biking:

Trails and Routes: New Mexico has a diverse range of biking trails and routes suitable for all skill levels. From paved urban paths to rugged mountain bike trails, there are options to suit your skills and preferences.

Mountain Biking: The state is well-known for its mountain biking opportunities. Trails in the Santa Fe National Forest, the Sandia Mountains near Albuquerque, and the Taos region provide thrilling rides with varying difficulty levels and breathtaking views.

Road Cycling: New Mexico's scenic highways and byways provide excellent routes for road cyclists. Enjoy the open roads, picturesque landscapes, and a sense of freedom as you pedal through charming towns and countryside.

Bike Rentals and Tours: If you don't have your own bike, there are bike rental shops throughout the state where you can find a suitable bike for your adventure. Additionally, guided biking tours are available, allowing you to explore the trails with experienced guides who can enhance your experience with their knowledge of the area.

Safety and equipment: When biking in New Mexico, it is critical to prioritize safety. Wear a helmet, use appropriate safety equipment, and be aware of traffic and trail conditions. Carry water, snacks, and any tools or spare parts you might need for bike maintenance.

Biking Events: Throughout the year, New Mexico hosts a variety of biking events and races, attracting cyclists from all over. Check local event calendars for upcoming races and rides if you want to participate or just watch.

Whether you prefer to explore on horseback or by bike, New Mexico has a plethora of opportunities to enjoy the great outdoors. With its diverse landscapes and well-maintained trails, you'll have a memorable adventure exploring the state's natural beauty on horseback or two wheels.

E. Rock Climbing

Outdoor enthusiasts will find rock climbing in New Mexico to be an exciting and challenging adventure. What you need to know about rock climbing in the state is as follows:

Diverse Climbing Areas: New Mexico has a wide range of climbing areas suitable for climbers of all skill levels. From sandstone cliffs to granite walls, there are a variety of rock formations to suit various climbing styles and techniques.

Enchanted Tower: The Enchanted Tower, located near Datil, is a popular climbing destination known for its unique volcanic rock formations. It has routes for both sport climbing and traditional climbing, with options for both beginners and more experienced climbers.

The Organ Mountains near Las Cruces provide a stunning backdrop for rock climbing. The granite cliffs and spires offer excellent trad and sport climbing opportunities. The area has a variety of routes ranging from moderate to difficult, making it suitable for climbers of all skill levels.

The Jemez Mountains in northern New Mexico are known for their volcanic rock formations, which attract climbers. The area has a mix of sports and traditional climbing routes of varying difficulty. The Jemez Mountains' scenic beauty and solitude add to the overall experience.

Sandia Mountains: The Sandia Mountains near Albuquerque is a popular rock climbing destination. The Sandias' granite cliffs offer a variety of climbing options, including multi-pitch routes and bouldering. The surrounding landscapes are breathtaking here.

Safety and Experience: In rock climbing, safety is of the utmost importance. It is critical to have proper climbing equipment, such as a helmet, harness, ropes, and climbing shoes. Climbing with a partner is recommended, and if you're a beginner, it's best to have prior experience or take guided instruction.

Guide Services: Hiring a professional guide service is a great option if you're new to rock climbing or unfamiliar with the area. They can provide instruction, equipment, and guidance to make climbing safe and enjoyable. Guides can also recommend the best climbing areas and routes for your skill level.

Weather Considerations: The weather in New Mexico varies depending on the season and location. It is critical to check the weather forecast before venturing out and to be prepared for changes in temperature and precipitation. Climbing can be dangerous in extreme weather conditions or when the rock is wet.

Leave No Trace: When rock climbing in New Mexico, follow the Leave No Trace principles. Respect the environment by packing out any trash or waste and minimizing your impact on the rock and surrounding vegetation. Contribute to the preservation of the natural beauty of the climbing areas for future generations.

Climbers of all levels will find rock climbing in New Mexico to be a thrilling and rewarding experience. The state's diverse climbing areas, stunning landscapes, and dedicated climbing community provide ample opportunities to challenge yourself while enjoying the beauty of the outdoors.

Chapter 12: Practical Information for new Mexico visitors

A. Currency and exchange rates

The US Dollar ($) is the currency of New Mexico and the rest of the United States. The US Dollar exchange rate fluctuates daily based on international currency markets. Exchange rates differ depending on where and how you exchange your money, such as at banks, currency exchange offices, or airports.

You can check with your bank or use reputable online currency converters that provide real-time rates to find the current exchange rates. Exchange rate information is also available on the websites and mobile apps of major financial institutions and currency exchange services.

It is critical to be aware of any fees or commissions that may be charged when exchanging currency. Some locations may offer lower rates but charge higher fees, so compare rates and fees to get the best deal.

Credit cards are widely accepted in New Mexico and can be used for the majority of transactions. However, it's always a good idea to keep some cash on hand for small purchases or in case you come across a business that doesn't accept cards.

Keep in mind that exchange rates and fees may vary, so do your homework and plan ahead of time to ensure you have the necessary funds in the local currency.

B. Health and safety tips

Stay hydrated: Because New Mexico has a dry climate, particularly in desert areas, it's critical to drink plenty of water to stay hydrated, even if you don't feel thirsty. Carry a water bottle and refill it regularly.

Protect yourself from the sun: Because New Mexico has a lot of sunshine, it's critical to protect your skin from harmful UV rays. Wear high-SPF sunscreen, a hat, sunglasses, and lightweight, breathable clothing that covers exposed skin.

Considerations for altitude: Some areas of New Mexico, particularly in the high mountain regions, have higher elevations. If you're not used to being at high altitudes, take it easy and give your body time to adjust. Stay hydrated and avoid strenuous physical activity until you feel better.

Carry necessary medications: If you require prescription medications, bring enough for the duration of your trip. If you're flying, keep them in their original packaging and pack them in your carry-on luggage.

Stay informed about weather conditions: The weather in New Mexico can be unpredictable, so stay up to date on weather forecasts, especially if you plan to engage in outdoor activities. Prepare for sudden temperature changes, especially in higher elevation areas.

Take proper hiking and outdoor safety precautions: If you intend to hike or explore outdoor areas, it is critical to take proper safety precautions. Inform someone of your plans, bring a map and compass, wear appropriate footwear and clothing, and keep an eye out for wildlife and potential hazards.

Be cautious of wildlife: New Mexico is home to a diverse range of wildlife, including snakes and insects. Learn about the local wildlife and take precautions to avoid encounters. Maintain a safe distance, do not disturb or feed wildlife, and take care where you step or place your hands in natural areas.

In national parks and recreational areas, follow the following safety guidelines: Follow park rules and guidelines if you visit New Mexico's national parks or recreational areas. Respect wildlife, stay on designated trails, dispose of trash properly, and exercise caution near cliffs, bodies of water, or other potentially hazardous areas.

Use insect repellent: Use insect repellent to protect yourself from bites in areas where insects, such as mosquitoes or ticks, may be present. In densely forested areas, wear long sleeves and pants.

General safety precautions should be taken: In New Mexico, as in any other travel destination, general safety precautions should be taken. Be aware of your surroundings, especially in cities, and take precautions to protect your belongings. Avoid leaving valuables visible by locking your car. It's also a good idea to keep a copy of your identification and emergency contact information on hand.

It's always a good idea to check with your doctor before traveling to New Mexico to ensure you have all of the necessary vaccinations and medications. Consider purchasing travel insurance to cover any medical emergencies or unexpected situations that may arise during your trip.

C. Communication and internet access

Here are some important points to remember about communication and internet access in New Mexico:

New Mexico has good mobile network coverage, with major providers such as AT&T, Verizon,

T-Mobile, and Sprint providing service throughout the state.

SIM Cards: If you're visiting from another country, you can get a local SIM card from a mobile network provider or an electronics store. This will provide you with a local phone number as well as a data plan for your stay.

If you intend to use your existing SIM card and plan from your home country, check with your mobile network provider about international roaming services and associated charges.

Wi-Fi is widely available in New Mexico, particularly in hotels, restaurants, cafes, and public areas such as airports and tourist information centers.

Internet Cafes: In major cities, internet cafes or co-working spaces provide fee-based internet access as well as additional services such as printing and scanning.

Public Libraries: Public libraries in New Mexico frequently offer free internet access to visitors, though you may need to register or show identification to use their computers.

Online Maps and Navigation: Online mapping services such as Google Maps are useful in New Mexico for navigating roads and finding points of interest. For areas with limited connectivity, downloading offline maps can be beneficial.

Internet speed varies depending on your location and service provider, with urban areas typically offering faster speeds than rural or remote areas.

Check with your mobile network provider about international roaming options and fees before your trip. If you need constant internet access, you should think about getting a local SIM card or a portable Wi-Fi device.

D. Useful phrases in Spanish

Here are some useful phrases in Spanish that can come in handy during your visit to New Mexico:

Hello - Hola

Good morning - Buenos días

Good afternoon - Buenas tardes

Good evening - Buenas noches

How are you? - ¿Cómo estás?

Thank you - Gracias

You're welcome - De nada

Please - Por favor

Excuse me - Disculpe

I'm sorry - Lo siento

Yes - Sí

No - No

Where is...? - ¿Dónde está...?

Can you help me? - ¿Puede ayudarme?

I don't understand - No entiendo

Do you speak English? - ¿Habla inglés?

How much does it cost? - ¿Cuánto cuesta?

I would like... - Me gustaría.

..

Cheers! - ¡Salud!

Goodbye - Adiós

Remember that many people in New Mexico are bilingual, and English is commonly spoken. However, using a few basic phrases in Spanish can show respect for the local culture and may be helpful in certain situations.

E. Recap of why New Mexico is a great travel destination

New Mexico is an excellent tourist destination for several reasons:

Natural Beauty: From deserts to mountains, New Mexico is home to a variety of landscapes and natural wonders, including Carlsbad Caverns,

White Sands National Park, and the Gila National Forest. Hiking, camping, skiing, and river rafting are all popular outdoor activities.

Rich Cultural Heritage: New Mexico is steeped in history and culture, with Native American, Hispanic, and European traditions all having a strong influence. Visitors can visit ancient Native American sites, historic towns and adobe architecture, and lively art and music scenes.

New Mexico is known for its vibrant art communities and galleries that showcase traditional and contemporary works. The state is also known for its distinct cuisine, which combines Native American, Mexican, and Spanish flavors in dishes such as green chile stew and enchiladas.

Festivals and Events: Throughout the year, New Mexico hosts numerous festivals and events, such as the Albuquerque International Balloon Fiesta, the

Santa Fe Indian Market, and the Gathering of Nations Powwow, which provide immersive cultural experiences.

Historic and cultural sites abound in New Mexico, from the ancient ruins of Chaco Culture National Historical Park to the historic adobe structures of Santa Fe and Taos.

Warm Hospitality: New Mexicans are known for their friendly nature and warm hospitality, which makes visitors feel welcome and at home during their stay.

Scenic Drives and Road Trips: The state provides breathtaking scenic drives such as the Enchanted Circle, Turquoise Trail, and High Road to Taos, which allow visitors to explore the stunning landscapes and charming towns at their own pace.

Outdoor Adventures: With its vast wilderness areas, New Mexico offers numerous opportunities for outdoor activities such as hiking, biking, rock climbing, and horseback riding.

Stargazing and Astronomy: With observatories and events dedicated to exploring the wonders of the night sky, New Mexico's clear skies and low light pollution make it an ideal destination for stargazing and astronomy enthusiasts.

Retreats for Spiritual and Healing: The state is home to spiritual and healing centers such as Taos and Ojo Caliente, which provide opportunities for relaxation, rejuvenation, and self-reflection.

Overall, New Mexico provides a distinct blend of natural beauty, cultural richness, outdoor adventures, and warm hospitality, making it an enticing destination for travelers looking for an immersive and unforgettable experience.

F. Useful apps and websites to enhance your New Mexico travel experience

Here are some useful apps and websites to enhance your New Mexico travel experience:

Google Maps: A popular navigation app that provides detailed maps, driving directions, and information on public transportation. It can assist you in navigating and exploring the state's attractions, as well as locating nearby amenities.

Airbnb or Booking.com: These platforms provide a variety of lodging options, such as hotels, vacation rentals, and bed and breakfasts. You can look for and book accommodations that meet your needs and budget.

Website of New Mexico (https://www.newmexico.org/): New Mexico's official tourism website offers detailed information on attractions, events, lodging, dining, and outdoor activities. It's an excellent resource for planning your trip and discovering lesser-known gems.

AllTrails is a well-known app for finding hiking, biking, and other outdoor trails. It offers trail maps, reviews, difficulty levels, and other useful information to help you explore the natural beauty of New Mexico.

Yelp or TripAdvisor: These platforms provide reviews and recommendations for New Mexico restaurants, attractions, and lodging. Based on other travelers' experiences, they can direct you to popular and hidden gems.

Weather Apps: Check the weather conditions and forecasts for your destination using apps such as AccuWeather, The Weather Channel, or your smartphone's native weather app. This can assist you in planning outdoor activities and packing accordingly.

GasBuddy: If you're going on a road trip to New Mexico, GasBuddy can help you find the closest and cheapest gas stations along the way. It displays real-time fuel prices as well as user reviews.

Uber or Lyft: These ride-sharing apps are available in New Mexico's major cities and offer convenient transportation options. You can request and pay for a ride through the app, making it simple to get around without a car.

New Mexico True TV YouTube Channel: This official YouTube channel features videos highlighting New Mexico's beauty, culture, and attractions. It can provide a visual preview of what to expect and inspire you to learn more about the state.

Websites of State and National Parks: If you plan to visit specific parks in New Mexico, check their official websites for information on admission fees, hiking trails, camping options, and any specific rules or regulations.

Remember to download and install these apps ahead of time, and keep an eye out for any updates or new apps that may be relevant to your specific interests or needs.

Printed in Great Britain
by Amazon

26350601R00136